The Journey of a Pilgrim

The Journey of a Pilgrim

John Bunyan

Brian H. Cosby

CF4•K

10 9 8 7 6 5 4 3

Copyright © 2009 Brian H. Cosby
Reprinted 2013 and 2016
Paperback ISBN: 978-1-84550-458-8
epub ISBN: 978-1-84550-891-3
mobi ISBN: 978-1-84550-892-0

Published by Christian Focus Publications,
Geanies House, Fearn, Tain,
Ross-shire, IV20 1TW, Scotland, U.K.
www.christianfocus.com; email: info@christianfocus.com

Cover design by Daniel van Straaten
Printed and bound by Nørhaven, Denmark

Throughout the text the Authorised Version of the Bible is used
for direct scripture quotes. In the *Thinking Further Topics* and *Life
Summary* the New International Version has been used.

This book is based on the life of John Bunyan. The incident where
John tells the story of the squirrel is not a direct story from him
but based on evidence that John told stories like this to the boys
in his village. There are other incidents throughout the book that
are fictionalised accounts, based on fact and that may well have
happened.

Contents

To Christian George,

a faithful friend, a suffering

servant, and a true pilgrim.

Raining Hard, Too Hard

'No!' John couldn't believe what he was hearing. He sat on his bed sobbing with his head buried in his hands. 'Why did she have to die?' He was only fifteen years old and his mother had become ill just a few days earlier.

Tears began streaming down his father's quivering cheeks. 'I don't know. I'm sorry, John. I am sure that God loves—'

'God does not love! He would not let her life end like this.'

'You mustn't say that,' Margaret gently responded. 'She is now with Him in heaven.' John's sister always had a way of softening his anger.

Still crying, John jumped up and ran outside. It was beginning to rain, but he didn't care.

He knew the place where his mother would be buried—the old Elstow churchyard. He had passed by it many times on the way to school or while playing with his friends. But this time would be different. No laughing or romping, just tears and a quiet respect of death.

Only a few friends attended the funeral. It was a cool morning and the fog rested heavy on the churchyard. Christopher Hall, the vicar of Elstow

Church, gave a warm eulogy and told those present not to mourn like those without hope, but to trust in the resurrection from the dead because Christ Jesus died and was raised to new life.

But John's little world was too shaken to accept it. 'Why would God allow Jesus to suffer and die? Does God not love His own Son?'

Sparks flew as Thomas Bunyan hammered the red-hot plough spike on the anvil. 'Almost finished,' he said with a feeling of accomplishment. He wiped the sweat from his brow and looked over at John who was quietly stacking a pile of freshly-chopped wood near the furnace. 'When you are finished with that, you can start on Mr Roberts' pot.'

John didn't say anything. It had only been a week since his mother's death and he was not in the mood to talk.

'Did you hear me, son?'

'Yes sir,' John replied, still concentrating on the wood pile.

The hot June afternoon sun beamed through the door of the shop, which made standing near the even hotter furnace almost unbearable. John and his father were tinkers, which meant that they worked with metal—repairing tools, crafting pots and welding various parts together.

Even when John was seven years old, he would pick up his father's hammer and pound pieces of metal while his father watched and instructed. There was something about stoking fire, hammering metal and getting dirty that made John feel like a man.

As Thomas cooled the plough spike in a trough of water, John reached down and picked up a large pot that had a dent in the side. Mr Roberts had dropped it off earlier and would be back soon to pick it up. 'This should be fairly easy,' he thought to himself. He grabbed the pot with a large scissor-like clamp and thrust it into the glowing furnace. He carefully set the red-hot pot on the horn of the anvil and reared back with his hammer.

'Aim well,' his father warned, stepping back a few feet.

John brought the hammer crashing down, shooting a flare of sparks all over the work area and all over John. 'Woaa,' John yelped, jumping back.

His father laughed. 'Well done. Now strike it again.'

Tinkers were not paid well. The Bunyan cottage had only two rooms, an attic and an attached work area off to the side. Neighbours frequently visited the shop to chat and to ask John's father to repair their broken tools.

'One day, you will have your own family to support,' his father said, taking John by the shoulder. 'You are doing well, but keep working. You still have much to learn.'

John glanced down. He felt like he was trapped. 'Why can't I do something different?' he wondered to himself. But he knew his father was right. If he was to support a family, he must carry on the family trade.

As daylight faded over the hills, the dark night's air sent a chill through the Bunyan household. John, Margaret, his younger brother William, and father gathered around the dinner table in silence. The absence of mother was difficult to bear and the reality of death was beginning to sink in.

Dinner time was especially difficult. Mother used to cheerfully hum while she cooked, sometimes breaking out into song. But now, the kitchen was still and quiet. Somehow, the joy and the warmth were gone. Although friends had provided the food, it wasn't mother's.

Father had already started eating when he noticed the three children sitting motionless staring at their food.

'Are you not eating tonight?' he asked with frustration, glancing around the table.

No one spoke.

'You should be grateful for the food on your plate. John, why don't you—'

'I'm not hungry!' With that John jumped up from the table and ran outside.

His bare feet felt the ground still warm from the hot summer sun. Stopping, he looked up into the night sky, trying to hold back his tears. 'God, if you're listening, please bring her back.' As he stood there, he was mysteriously comforted. Millions of glittering stars filled the sky and the cool evening breeze gave him a sense of peace. But it didn't stop the tears.

He heard some footsteps on the grass behind him. 'John?' a soft voice gently called.

'Oh, hello Margaret,' he said taking a deep breath. John loved his sister. They had grown up playing together. When they were younger, they would build dams in the creek and catch crayfish. But now, she was closer than a playmate.

'Why don't you come back in and eat?'

'I can't. It's not like it used to be.'

'I know, but it's hard on father and he needs us.' They stood motionless—silently looking up at the twinkling bright stars. Orion and the Pleiades were especially clear. It was quiet, too quiet.

'Margaret,' John finally began, still gazing into the night sky. 'Do you think that God really loves us?'

'Of course,' Margaret answered rather puzzled by the question. 'Don't you?'

'I think so. Sometimes, though, I feel like…'

'Like what?'

'Like everything that we've been taught in the Bible is nothing but a way to keep us out of trouble.'

'Well, it sure didn't keep you out of trouble growing up!' They both laughed.

All of the sudden, Margaret's laugh turned into a wheezing cough.

'Are you all right?' John asked.

'I'm fine. It is only a little cough coming on. John, now is not the time to be thinking about such things. Mother has just died and I heard that it is not good to doubt in times like these. Besides, she used to always tell us that God has big plans for our lives, remember?'

It was strange how much Margaret was like their mother—gentle, compassionate, full of wisdom. John was glad she was there.

'Perhaps you are right.'

Just then, they heard a call from the house. 'John. Margaret. It's time to get ready for bed.'

'Don't worry about it,' she said looking at John. She smiled. 'Race you back!'

A couple of weeks later, John woke up early one morning. He could see a faint golden sunlight coming through the window and feel a chill in the air. Even in the summer mornings were cool.

He looked over at Margaret sleeping. With so few rooms all the children had to bunk up together in the one bedroom. John was used to hearing strange noises during the night but this morning something wasn't right. Looking closer, he could see that Margaret's face was glistening with sweat.

'Margaret?' John whispered. He didn't want to wake up William. 'Margaret,' he whispered again a little louder. She did not answer. Springing out of the bed, he ran over to her side. Her forehead burned with fever and he could hear her moaning.

'What's wrong?' he said frightened. 'Are you all right?'

She faintly mumbled a few words, but he couldn't understand her.

With mounting fear, John yelled for his father, but Mr Bunyan was already racing to the bed with a damp rag and a bowl of water. He had heard her moans just before John awoke. John couldn't help but think that if mother was here she would know what to do.

John stood up, his chin quivering. Margaret looked so pale and helpless.

Her 'little' cough had grown worse during the two weeks following their conversation under the stars. Before the day was over, Margaret would join her mother in the Elstow Churchyard. The year was 1644. She was fourteen years old.

The village of Elstow was located about two miles south of the town of Bedford, which was always bustling with traders and merchants. The Bunyan cottage stood only a few yards from the Elstow parish boundary and was almost as close to Bedford as to Elstow church. John would roll a wooden cart loaded with his father's pots, pans and other metal wares through the streets looking for prospective customers.

One afternoon, as he travelled north from Elstow, he stopped on the bridge overlooking the Great Ouse River. The river began in Northamptonshire and flowed 149 miles to the town of King's Lynn, running straight through the middle of Bedford. As he looked down the row of large oak trees lining its banks he felt a warm breeze blowing across the water. John closed his eyes and recalled the summer days when he and his friends would play in the river.

'Get moving!' barked a gruff baritone voice.

Startled, John whirled around. 'I...I...I'm sorry, sir,' he stammered.

A massive man with a bushy brown beard and dirty hands trudged by, carrying a large bundle of hay strapped over his shoulder. His type was a common site during the summer months, which were a time of haymaking and sheep-shearing. Tall grass was cut and spread on the ground to dry. It was then gathered and piled into haystacks to be sold in the market as food for the livestock. The summer market was very different from the spring market when the streets smelled of horse manure used for fertilizer. John liked summer much better because he could take a quick swim off the river's bank when nobody was looking.

On the north side of the bridge stood St Paul's— a large stone church with a central tower and tall pointy spire. John had always marvelled at the size of the building. 'I wonder how long it took to build?' he thought to himself. On Sundays, he could hear its eight large bells ringing all the way from Elstow. He was always intrigued with the ringing bells and pictured himself secretly climbing up the tower at night and ringing the bells himself. He chuckled, imagining the whipping that mother would have given him, had he actually done such a thing.

The church scared John—not so much the building, but what was preached. The pastor of the church in Elstow would describe the great Day of Judgment when the Book of Life would be opened and all who belonged to Christ Jesus—all whose names were written in the Book—would be eternally saved from the fires of hell.

'I'm never going to be good enough to be saved,' John thought frowning. He stood gazing up at the church spire for a while.

'What's this?' an older man with greasy grey hair suddenly asked, looking puzzled at a long curved sharp metal object that was hanging from John's cart.

'It's a scythe,' John answered. He could tell that the man was not well-educated. 'You attach it to a long wooden pole to cut tall grass or brush.'

The man sniffed. 'Looks more like some sort of weapon if you ask me.'

'Well, I'm not asking you, so put it down!'

Astonished at John's impertinence, the old man threw down the piece of metal. 'Who do you think you are to speak to me like that?' he demanded.

'John Bunyan, sir,' he replied with a confident smile. For a reason he didn't understand, John actually enjoyed making strangers mad. He knew it was wrong, but he didn't care.

'Well, I've never—'

'Good day,' John interrupted, picking up the end of the cart and continuing to roll it along St Paul's square. As John pushed the cart, people could hear its rickety frame and banging pots from some distance—he didn't have to do much advertising.

He passed by the Bedford schoolhouse which stood on the southwest corner of St Paul's square. He would occasionally see boys his age running out and wrestling in the street. 'I wish I still went to school,' he thought to himself. He had gone to school briefly when he was younger, but his father couldn't afford to send him beyond grammar school. In spite of this, he learned to read and write—skills he would enjoy and use the rest of his life.

Clouds were beginning to ominously roll over the schoolhouse from the west. If he quickened his pace, he could reach home before the approaching storm. Even in the summer, getting wet could result in fatal illness. He swung the cart around and hurried back toward Elstow.

It felt strange when, a few weeks later, John's father brought home a woman to marry—'Ann,' they called her. She was a warm motherly figure, but certainly not his mother and never would be.

John sat curled up on his bed next to the front window of their home watching the night rain settle into puddles on the street outside. Candles were flickering from the house across the street. It looked as though some sort of celebration was going on inside—people were laughing and singing. He stared at the puddles again. There was no celebration in his home.

Lightning raced across the sky. 'Boom!' Thunder shook the timbers that supported the walls of the little cottage.

'How could father get over my mother so quickly?' he wondered, letting a slow tear splash on his knee. He felt as though his new step-mother was trying to erase the warm memories of his real mother. He felt as though his father didn't care about him. 'He could have at least talked to me about getting married before he actually did,' he thought still staring at the growing puddles.

He remembered Margaret too—his childhood playmate. 'What's happening to my family?' he muttered under his breath.

The rain was coming down hard, too hard. It was pounding John's little world.

'No one is going out tonight,' came a voice from behind him.

Startled, John jerked his head around. His father was holding a five-pronged candlestick. The little flames danced from the draft blowing through the crack around the front door.

John didn't say anything. He wiped his cheeks with his shirt sleeve and gazed back out the window.

'Get some sleep,' his father said, walking away.

'Will I ever see mother again?' John asked himself.

His eyes scanned the dark night sky as if he were trying to find her. He wondered if she was in heaven. Neither of his parents had discussed the Christian faith very much with him. Like most families in Elstow, they attended church, but their daily lives usually did not reflect a deep Christian conviction.

'Will I go to heaven?' he wondered, looking again up to the sky.

Suddenly, his eyes felt heavy. It was strange how crying always seemed to make him sleepy. He slowly meandered over to his bed and crawled under the patch-work quilt made by his grandmother years ago. 'Boom!' Thunder ripped through John's dreams like death through his family—

'Get away!' John screamed. The fiery red eyes followed him like a hawk. 'Please, don't take me to hell!' As the demon chased him out into the night, he could hear the hoarse breath and summon over his shoulder—'John, you're coming with me!'

'No!' John screamed. He could feel the demonic presence closing in on him.

The demon didn't let up. 'You can't run. Don't you understand? This is where you will spend eternity!'

His lungs burning, John stumbled to a stop and slumped over. 'Get away,' he cried. 'Get away...Get away...Get away...'

His own voice startled him awake. Soaked in sweat and gasping for breath, he sat up. 'Just a dream,' he whispered to himself as his panic subsided. Thoughts of hell-fire would often torment his soul—the burning and the chains.

John feared the great 'Day of Judgment' about which his preacher had warned the congregation. He would have frightening dreams and dreadful visions of hell and the day when Jesus would separate His people from the rest. He felt that he was certainly part of the 'rest.'

The next morning, John walked out into the morning fog, making footprints on the dew-covered ground. Two streams flowed near the Bunyan cottage, which were now overflowing from the night's violent storm.

He strolled down to one of the streams at the bottom of a gently-sloping hill opposite the street and knelt beside the water. He saw his reflection staring back at him. 'Not a beautiful sight,' he thought. He plunged his hands into the water and splashed his face. The coolness on his skin refreshed his spirit, reminding him of when he and Margaret would run to this stream and splash each other until one fell in. 'It was not that long ago,' he remembered. Taking a deep breath, he stood up, prepared to face another long day.

With troubled souls and tragedy at home, the summer of 1644 was finally coming to an end. The fields were abundant with vegetables and barley. John was beginning to embrace his new step-mother as part of the family. He still missed his mother and Margaret, but found that time is a great healer of grief and pain. All seemed quiet and peaceful. Nevertheless, something lurked beneath the calm. John could hear faint explosions in the distance—cannons and muskets. Parliament was fighting King Charles I and war would soon find its way to his doorstep.

Guns, Smoke and God

The twilight hour didn't help the confusion. People raced back and forth in a panic and John didn't know what to do. He froze when he heard the growing sound of a troop of horses stampeding straight for Bedford. The clinks of metal swords and the pounding of hooves sounded like rolling thunder coming across the hills.

'Lights!' shrieked a scared older woman.

John looked. A line of torches spread across the horizon over the houses. He stood on the northwest corner of St Paul's square next to the church. It was his sixteenth birthday—28 November—and he and his brother William had been celebrating at a friend's house on Silver Street, one block up from the square. They ran outside when they heard the shouting.

As John stood watching the dark silhouettes approach, painful memories of last year's raid flashed through his mind. Almost exactly one year earlier, in October 1643, a division of Royalists under Sir Lewis Dyve stormed into Bedford, plundered the town and took a band of defenders as prisoners.

But now the riders had turned down Well Street and were coming straight at John. However, to his surprise, he heard cheering from the townspeople. 'Cheering?' he said confused. As they approached St Paul's square, he could see their matchlock muskets, their tightly pulled-back hair and their red and grey Parliamentary uniforms. What a relief! It wasn't the Royalists after all!

They stopped directly in front of the church and a few dismounted. A swarm of people gathered around, intrigued by the evening visit.

'Hear, hear, men of Bedford,' suddenly blared a deep and confident voice. John saw a large barrel-chested man with a feather sticking up out of his hat drawing his horse out in front of the others. 'The Cavaliers have encamped fifty miles to the west and Parliament has voted a levy for this town. All able men of at least sixteen years of age are hereby called to arms.'

John felt the fruitcake he had just gobbled turn over in his stomach. 'I turned sixteen...today,' he thought to himself with his eyes getting wider and wider.

'Brother, does that mean you?' came a young voice behind him. William had followed him outside and heard the Lieutenant-Colonel's call.

John didn't answer. He knew his time had come.

They stationed John at Newport Pagnell, about fifteen miles west of Bedford. The garrison there was an important midpoint between the Royalist armies in the west and the Parliamentary armies in the east.

King Charles I had not only tried to demand that all the realm use the *Book of Common Prayer* and the Anglican form of church government, he had also tried to raise taxes on the people without Parliamentary consent. The double blow gave Parliament the motivation it needed to raise an army against the king and Charles responded by raising his royal standard at Nottingham on 22 August 1642.

Two years later, John found himself struggling over whether or not fighting his king was even right. 'Was it not God who set the king over us as ruler and protector,' he thought to himself. Although something didn't seem right about fighting his king, he believed in the Parliamentary cause.

A lot of boys his age were also stationed at Newport Pagnell. They had come from the neighbouring counties of Huntingdon, Cambridge, Hertfordshire and Suffolk. He recognized some of them from Elstow and Bedford. They were all the same boys he had grown up with but they were soldiers now and in uniform.

One night John sat on his cot in the barracks looking at the red and grey uniform he would be wearing the next day. The sword they issued to him was long and curved and appeared to have some blood stains between the crevices in the handle. 'I wonder who this sword killed,' he thought. He put his hand around the grip and quickly pulled it out of the sheath, making a high-pitched ring. The long metal blade reflected the flames dancing in the fire.

'Do you know how to use that?' asked a tall noble-looking man from across the other side of the room.

'Yes sir,' John affirmed. It was a lie. He had never wielded a sword before in his life, but he wasn't going to let this gentleman start making fun of him, especially in front of the other well-seasoned soldiers reading and talking around the room.

'Well, we shall make you better. There is no time to spare so you shall start your training in the morning. Good night.' With that the man stretched out on his cot and rolled over facing the outside wall.

It was a cold night. John lay down and pulled a wool blanket up around his head. He thought about the night he left Bedford. His father was angry, not so much with him, but with Parliament for voting for the levy. His father actually sided with the king and with the Royalist army, but mainly out of fear. Bedfordshire was almost entirely in favour of Parliament. 'Father is in the wrong place,' John thought to himself smiling.

A barrage of musket-fire ripped through the cool morning air. The Major paced back and forth yelling at the lined formation of young nervous soldiers. 'Not good enough! Again!'

John thrust the gun to his side and waited for the command.

'Prime and load!'

He made a quarter turn to the right, at the same time bringing the gun up to the priming position. The musket fired a spherical lead bullet propelled by a small explosion of black gunpowder. A clamp on top of the gun held a slow-burning match that, when the trigger was pulled, would lower it into a small pan igniting the powder. It was accurate only to about 150 feet.

A well-trained soldier could fire up to three rounds a minute in dry weather. Hard rain, however, made it nearly impossible to keep the match lit. Most of the time, then, the soldier would turn the gun around and use it as an expensive club.

'Draw ramrods,' bellowed the Major. 'Present.'

John put the butt of the gun against his shoulder and aimed at the straw-filled target resembling a Cavalier infantryman.

'Fire!'

The kick almost knocked John off his feet. He could barely make out the little hole in the blue cloth covering the target through the thick cloud of smoke. 'I hit it!' he blurted out in surprise.

'It is different when it is a real person,' the man next to him said, who smelled like he had been sleeping with the horses. 'Soon enough, you shall see.'

Two weeks later, Lieutenant Colonel Richard Cokayne, John's immediate superior, walked into the barracks. 'All of you will report to central command in the morning. John, that includes you.'

John had developed blisters on his feet from all of the formation drills over the last few days and he was cutting one open with his knife, allowing it to drain.

'Yes sir, Lieutenant Colonel,' he affirmed.

The next morning, he and 224 others, including Lieutenant Colonel Cokayne, met up with Sir Samuel Lake, the commander over the Newport Pagnell garrison. Lake was a Presbyterian, which meant he believed in a representative-style church government ruled by a session of elders or overseers—a government extremely popular in Scotland. Scotland had joined together with Parliament in what they called 'The Solemn League and Covenant' in 1643, which paved the way for Scotland to send nearly 20,000 troops into England to fight with Parliament against the king.

Lake was an honorable man and committed to God. He had a deep-felt belief that he was fighting against tyranny and the forces of evil.

'Today we have received word that a regiment is planning a surprise attack here on Newport Pagnell and we are going to stop them!' His speech was strong and unwavering. 'The king wants to take away your voice and representation. He wants your money to fund his wars. Well, he will have to fight through us!'

His words elicited courage in the hearts of the men standing around. John could feel the excitement and camaraderie growing by the second. His own heart pounded with pride. 'Will you fight?'

'Yes!' yelled the band of men in unison. John felt that he was part of something great. Immediately, soldiers mounted horses and others grabbed pikes*.

* 14-foot (4.2672 metre) wooden poles for repelling cavalry attacks

Still others, like John, grabbed a musket. It all happened so fast.

He filed into formation and off they went, marching west to meet up with the Royalist regiment. The pikemen in the front of the line had their long pikes sticking straight up in the air and would occasionally get snagged in a branch of an overhanging tree.

After almost two hours of marching, they took a break. John took a big gulp of water and wiped the remnant on his coat sleeve. It was now 13 December 1644 and a blistering cold wind was blowing across the fields and pastures. Surprisingly, he was quite warm. Marching was a good way to fight off the cold in the winter, though it could be very dangerous. If you stopped, any sweat built up from walking would quickly start cooling the body off—sometimes too much, leading to hypothermia.

Many died from disease and hypothermia. In fact, during the English Civil War, more people died from disease and sickness than from actually being killed in battle. John knew all too well this danger of sickness. He had seen its effects on both his mother and sister.

All of the sudden, John heard a string of explosions and a soldier next to him screamed out in pain, hitting the ground. Afraid, John hit the ground trying to figure out where the shots came from. He looked to his right and saw a line of muskets resting on a rock wall not more than 130 feet away. It was a surprise attack.

Before he knew what was happening, Lieutenant Colonel Cokayne began barking out orders and the men started forming lines.

'Present,' he shouted.

John quickly jumped in line formation and aimed his gun at the Cavalier regiment behind the rock wall. His hands were shaking and he could feel his heart pounding in his ears.

'Fire!'

Flames shot out from the ends of the muskets creating a dense wall of smoke. Immediately, some of the men drew swords and others turned their muskets around and charged straight at the enemy behind the wall.

John reached into a leather pouch dangling at his side and pulled out a musket ball. He primed, loaded and rammed the cartridge down the length of the barrel as he nervously hunched over trying to dodge shots whizzing by. Through the smoke, he could make out a Cavalier fighting hand-to-hand with the tall noble-looking man—the man he had talked with in the barracks!

He took aim at the blue uniform and put his finger on the trigger. But for some reason, he couldn't do it. He took a deep breath and aimed again when all of a sudden the butt of a musket slammed into his thigh knocking him to the ground. A large man reared back and swung right at John's chest, but John thrust his gun into the air blocking the blow. He tried to scramble out of the way, but the man grabbed his sling and sent a couple of fists into John's ribs.

'Kaboom!' The deafening blast sent glowing embers all over both of them. John felt the man on top of him go limp and then rolled over with a fresh bullet-hole through his abdomen.

'Are you all right?' came a young voice through the smoke.

John looked up, trying to reorient himself to what just happened. A boy, about his age, holding a musket stood a few feet away—dirty and with a cut across his forehead.

'Are you all right?' the boy asked again.

John sat up, gasping for breath. 'Yes, I'm fine.'

'He just about finished you,' the boy said with a smile. 'Here.' He reached out his hand toward John.

John pulled himself up and brushed himself off. 'Thank you.'

'The name's Dorsett—James Dorsett.'

'John Bunyan. I am very pleased to meet you,' he said with hands still clasped.

John scanned the scene and realized that the Cavaliers were retreating.

'Shall we follow them?' John asked not knowing whether to take a shot with his primed gun.

'No. Sir Lake is a man of principle. He would never finish off a defeated army.'

The march back to Newport Pagnell was quiet except for the sound of footsteps and beating drums. But even the drums had a dreary and somber tone.

John seemed lost in his own world. It was his first encounter with the Royalist army and the images of wounded and dying men weighed heavily on his mind. With every step, he could feel pain shooting down his leg. It didn't feel broken, but the musket blow would certainly leave a bruise.

That night, Sir Samuel Lake walked into his barracks. 'Men.' He paused and removed his hat. 'I want you to know that you fought with courage and bravery. Forty three of our brothers have fallen and another sixty are injured. It has been a day of tragedy. But God, in His providence, has brought us through victoriously and has refined us with fire. Pray for the families and pray for our cause. Let us be strong and trust in God even in this hour of loss.'

Lake had a way of putting things in perspective. His faith in God gave him a peace that John didn't understand. It reminded him of the stories of Oliver Cromwell, who would lead his cavalry, called Ironsides, into battle, confident that God was with him and would give the enemy into his hand.

'I wish I had faith like that,' John thought.

Some of the men in the barracks began praying together. John wanted to join them, but felt out of place. Suddenly he felt a firm, but gentle hand on his shoulder. John turned around. It was Thomas Ford, the chaplain stationed at Newport Pagnell. He was, like Lake, a Presbyterian.

'You seem troubled, my friend. May I sit down?'

John scooted over on his cot. 'Please.'

Ford was a short man with dirty-blonde hair. He wore a black cloak with a white collar extending down his chest. There was something about him that made John feel welcomed and at peace.

'What's your name?' Ford asked calmly.

'John Bunyan, sir. My family is from Elstow.'

Ford sat up and closed his eyes as though he was trying to remember something. 'Oh, right. Your father works as a tinker, right?'

'Yes sir. I work—well, I used to work—with him.'

'Tell me, how many years are you?'

John glanced unconsciously around the room. 'I turned sixteen not more than two weeks ago. I was called to arms on my birthday.'

'What a birthday present,' Ford said with a low-pitched chuckle. 'Tell me, how is your faith?'

John paused and looked down, frowning. 'To be honest, sir, I...I don't really know. I mean, I go to church.'

'But what about your personal faith?' he asked with greater intention. He looked at John as if he were trying to peer into his soul.

After a long pause, John finally blurted out. 'I'm scared of hell. I always have been. I don't think I'm good enough to go to heaven.' John couldn't believe he was actually telling this stranger what he had always kept hidden.

'You are right about that,' Ford said with another chuckle.

'About what?'

'That you're not good enough to go to heaven.'

John was confused. Wasn't the chaplain supposed to give words of comfort and hope? 'What do you mean?'

'The fact is, my friend, nobody is good enough to go to heaven. But if you put your faith in Jesus Christ as Lord and Saviour, you shall be clothed in His righteousness and God lets you into heaven, not because you are a good person, but because Christ is your righteousness. You are counted "not guilty" because Christ has taken the punishment of your sin upon himself.'

John was intrigued. For the first time, he wanted to know more about God's love in Christ.

'Put your faith in God, my friend. He holds great plans for your life.'

Chaplain Ford patted him on the back, stood up and walked out of the barracks.

Still thinking, John looked down at his wet leather boots. 'Christ is my righteousness? He has taken the punishment of my sin?' He liked the chaplain, but felt very distant from his message…and distant from God.

The winter of 1644–45 was long and cold. The following May, John found himself fighting under

Lieutenant Colonel Charles O'Hara. Now, the flowers were in full bloom and the robins were chirping in the bright-green trees.

But the birds weren't the only sound in the air. Canons blasted the outer homes of Aylesbury, a small town twenty miles south of Newport Pagnell. The Cavaliers had captured the town and Lieutenant Colonel O'Hara was determined to take it back.

John stood watch on the right side of the Parliamentary division facing Aylesbury. It was his duty to report any sign of approaching horse that might try to outflank O'Hara's company. They were laying siege to the town in hopes that the Royalist army would flee.

Every now and then, one of his comrade's would be shot from stray musket fire, usually from a window in one of the homes in the town. It was a difficult task and it had lasted almost three days.

For his part, John was keeping watch through the night. The moon provided just enough light to play tricks on his mind. At one point, around 2 a.m., John thought he saw a troop of cavalry trying to secretly skirt around the right flank.

'Horse!' John yelled, pointing out in front of him. The row of soldiers lying next to him barely moved.

'I see horse!' John yelled a bit louder.

The men grumbled in irritation. 'Be quiet young lad.'

By that point, John realized that he was just seeing things in the night. 'Maybe I should get some sleep,' he thought to himself.

Suddenly, he heard a familiar voice. 'John?' He turned around. It was James Dorsett, the boy who saved his life last December. 'You should get some sleep. Let me stand your post for a while.'

John liked the idea. 'Are you sure?'

'Yes, I'm sure. I will trade with you in a few hours.'

John stepped down from the wooden platform used to scout out enemy movements and rolled out a wool blanket that he carried with him.

Falling asleep wasn't as easy as he thought. The sporadic, but constant shooting kept John awake. The blasts were far enough apart to let him begin dozing off, but close enough together to keep him from falling completely asleep. But he tried anyway.

Not even an hour had passed when John heard a thud hit the ground. He jumped up looking in the direction of the sound. In the moonlight, he could see the wooden platform empty and James lying at its base—face down.

'James?' John questioned softly, getting on his hands and knees.

He did not answer.

John quickly crawled over to the body and turned him over. James was dead. A musket ball had hit him in the side of his head and his hair was wet with blood.

Without making a sound, John began to cry. 'That should have been me,' he thought still holding James in his arms.

'God, I hate you!' John finally blurted out loud in anger.

In the summer of 1647, Parliament disbanded O'Hara's company and John went home. Parliament would go on to win the war and eventually execute King Charles. For the first time England would be ruled by a Parliamentary government with Oliver Cromwell as England's 'Lord Protector.'

John's string of misfortunes—the death of his mother, sister and friend—made him bitter toward God. Any openness toward God's love closed shut. Now, he did what he wanted to do and he didn't care what anybody thought. As far as he was concerned, the church was full of hypocrites and liars and he would have no part of it!

Chief of Sinners!

John shot out past the defender and kicked the ball through the bushes. 'Point! You're too slow!' he yelled looking at the nine-year-old defeated opponent.

The young boy had been pushed around all afternoon and was fed up with all of John's smart comments. 'You cheated!' he finally blurted with water welling up in his eyes.

'Did not! You just can't play with us men. It is three to one, our lead.' John retrieved the ball and dribbled it back to the middle of the field. It was a hot September Sunday afternoon and the group of boys had found a pasture outside of Elstow where no one could see them. It was illegal to play games on Sunday.

'I do not think we should be out here,' said Thomas Bray, one of John's friends who lived down the street. He looked over both shoulders as though he thought someone was watching.

'Why? Are you afraid?' John teased with a half smile.

Thomas peered back at John. 'No, I'm not.'

'Well, what are you waiting for? It's your ball,' John said, kicking the ball to Thomas.

Thomas paused, took the ball and began racing down the field with John following in close pursuit. John reached his foot in front of Thomas to steal the ball when all of the sudden their feet entangled and Thomas went flying through the air, landing hard on the dry dusty ground. Immediately, Thomas jumped up, ran straight at John and landed a fist across his face—and down they went, swinging. Before long, all of the boys piled on to break up the fight, eventually pulling the two apart.

'What is your problem?' John yelled with blood coming out of his nose.

'My problem? Why do you always play so rough and trip me like that?' With that Thomas walked over to the ball, picked it up and punted it as hard as he could. The ball sailed through the air and landed on the other side of a short rock wall next to the tailor's shop—rolling straight into the arms of Ms Margaret Whiteside, the meanest lady in town. The boys froze.

'What do you think you are doing on the Lord's Sabbath?' she said, seething with anger.

They all looked at John. He was the one who had persuaded them to play in the first place. 'I'm sorry, Ms Whiteside,' he stammered, his voice cracking. 'We just came over to play an innocent—'

'Innocent?' she exclaimed. 'You think fooling around on the Sabbath is pleasing to God? Go home, all of you. Go home!'

The boys took off, some running toward Bedford and others toward Elstow.

When John arrived at home, he was hoping his father wasn't around. He quietly unlatched the back door and slowly walked in. As he tip-toed across the wood floor to the front room where he slept, he heard another set of steps behind him.

'John, where have you been?' His father had seen him coming down the street. 'Were you playing over behind the tailor's shop again?'

John wiped the remaining blood on his sleeve and turned around. 'Yes, sir.'

'You will have no dinner tonight. Go to your room.'

John turned, walked to his room and closed the door.

The next morning, John got up early to finish a few projects in his father's shop. Although the suffering of war had hardened his heart toward God, it allowed him to appreciate his job as a tinker. At least he wasn't cold and wet in some open field waiting for the enemy to take a shot at him. His father worked in the shop too, but not as much as he used to. He 'let' John take over much of his work so that John would grow and develop as a tinker in his own right.

As he knelt down to stoke the coals of the fire, it brought back memories of stoking the fires in his barracks at Newport Pagnell. It was hard to believe that it had only been three months since his company disbanded. Parliament had control of London and, under the leadership of Oliver Cromwell, had issued a series of laws to bring a moral reformation to the whole of England.

Most people rallied around Cromwell, but John didn't understand it. As far as he was concerned, Cromwell had taken away his fun. He wasn't allowed to dance or play games. And only four months earlier, in June 1647, Parliament outlawed the celebration of Christmas, Easter and Lent!

'They need to loosen up,' he thought, still stoking the fire.

A family was supposedly coming by that day to pick up a set of pots they had dropped off the week before. He didn't know where the family was from, but he knew they were not from Elstow. Everybody knew everybody in Elstow and everybody certainly knew John, or at least his disrupting reputation over the last few months.

He took the large scissor-like clamp and stuck the last of the pots into the fire. He waited until the metal was glowing red and then put it on the horn of the anvil. As he hammered away, the pot soon took on its final shape.

Suddenly, he heard a young female voice from the door of the shop. 'Mr Bunyan?'

'Just a minute. I'm al...most...finished,' he called pounding the metal between each syllable. 'There.' He stood up and turned around to greet his visitor.

When he saw her, he couldn't believe his eyes. She was the most beautiful girl he had ever seen. Her long wavy brown hair draped over her petite shoulders. It seemed like time itself stopped—though it might have been his heart.

'Are you Mr Bunyan?' she said with a tender smile.

John was in awe. Her deep brown eyes wouldn't let his blink. 'Yes…I mean, no. What I'm trying to say is…my name is John and this is my father's shop.' He felt like he was stuttering and wanted to run before he made a fool of himself.

She bowed, giving a curtsy. 'Pleasure to meet you, John.'

Though he didn't say it, it was a greater pleasure for him. 'Nice to meet you too.'

'I have come to pick up some pots for my father, who is waiting outside,' she explained, pointing out the door.

'Perfect! I've just finished the last one. Let me cool it off first.' John took the pot with his clamp and plunged it into the large wooden trough filled with water, making a hiss. He stacked the pots, one inside of the other, and wrapped them in a brown piece of hessian cloth.

She placed two shillings on the counter and grabbed the stack of pots. Looking at John, she gave another curtsy. 'Thank you.' Before John could say anything, she turned and walked out of the door.

'Wait!' he yelled, running after her. He stopped when he saw a tall, thin man dressed in black sitting on a carriage. 'Good day, sir.' He realized it was her father. John looked back at her. 'May I have your name?'

'Mary.' She smiled and then climbed into the carriage.

'Mary,' he said to himself as they pulled away, apparently heading toward Bedford. 'I hope to meet you again,' he whispered, but his words disappeared into the empty air.

He walked back into the shop. Next on the list was fixing a bent sword for 'Mr...' He couldn't quite read his father's writing. The sword was propped against the wall near the woodpile and was clearly in need of repair.

He put his hand around the grip of the handle and swung it up in front of his face. It was similar to the sword he had in the army—except for the blood stains. He was about to hold the bent part in the fire when his friend Thomas walked in.

'Good morning.'

John looked over his shoulder. 'Up early, I see.'
'Indeed. I am supposed to be on my way to Bedford for mother. She wants me to purchase John Milton's book, *Areopagitica*, as a gift for my grandfather. I think the book is about our right to write and publish without first having to obtain a license. Have you heard of it?'

'I think so.' John didn't read very much. He used to read the Bible when he was younger, but it had been a while.

'Anyway, I wanted to know if you would like to go to Moot Hall later tonight, after your parents go to bed. You can bring your brother too if you want.' Moot Hall was a brick and timber building with a projecting upper story in the middle of Elstow.

'You're going dancing tonight?' John asked. 'With who?'

Thomas smiled and leaned on the front counter. 'Girls—who else? What say you?'

'Who do you think you're talking to? Of course.'

'Very good. I'll meet you in front of the tailor's shop at ten.' Thomas bolted out of the door and turned toward Bedford.

'I wonder if Mary would come to Moot Hall?' John wondered. He frowned. 'I don't even know where she lives.' Still holding the sword in his hand, he knelt down and stuck it in the fire.

That night, John and Thomas met as planned and started walking toward Moot Hall. It was a full moon and there seemed to be a million stars out— they could actually see quite well. The Hall had a large wood floor and was usually used as either town storage or to settle public disputes. Tonight, however, was a different story. John was surprised that none of his friends' parents knew about what went on late at night. It wasn't every night, only occasionally. 'Maybe that's why parents didn't know,' he thought.

They skipped with excitement across the village green feeling the rush of doing something they knew they shouldn't be doing. As they approached the Hall, they heard a faint sound of music and people laughing.

'Music!' John yelped and the two of them started sprinting toward the door. When they walked in, they saw the room full of young people dancing, smoking pipes and playing a variety of musical instruments. It was a community folk dance—a community of young rebels at that! They did see, however, a couple of middle-aged men who were just sitting in a corner smoking pipes.

John caught the eye of one of them. 'Maybe we'll be safe if we get caught. They might have authorized this,' motioning his head toward the two gentlemen.

The music was a mixture of old folk tunes played by the tabor (a single snare drum), hurdy gurdies (which resembled fiddles) and crumhorns (which sounded like bagpipes). John didn't waste any time. He jumped right in and started dancing all around the room as though it was the first time he had ever experienced so much fun.

'Come on, Thomas!' he yelled from across the room. Thomas joined in and, before long, the room was full of sweaty boys and girls—all having the time of their lives.

But before they had been there even twenty minutes, someone let out a shriek. All heads turned and the music stopped. The side of the wall had caught on fire from a set of candles and the flames were beginning to lap up the sap-filled oak beams. While some of the boys grabbed potato sacks and tried to suppress the flames, others hurried out of the Hall screaming. John and Thomas ran out too.

When they stopped and looked back at the Hall, it seemed like the fire was under control. But now the town was awake and John wasn't going to get caught again! 'Come on, let's get out of here!'

The two ran straight out into a field behind a row of houses and turned north, running parallel to the main road that went through Elstow. By now, they could hear older adults yelling and making a fuss on the other side of the houses and John felt a sense of relief that he wasn't in the mix of it. When they reached the back of the old Elstow church, they stopped out of breath.

'That was close,' Thomas said as he bent over gasping for breath. 'Too close. I mean, one minute more and we—'

'Shhhh...,' John whispered.

Thomas looked up. John was staring at the top of the church steeple. 'John, what is it?'

'What do you say we climb the steeple and ring the bells?'

Thomas looked at the bells and then looked back at John. 'Are you out of your mind?'

'The town is already awake anyway, and if we climb down fast enough, we can make it to my back door in no time. When father wakes and walks out the front, we can slip through the back and give him the impression that we just woke up too.'

It sounded like a plan. 'Fine, but this is your idea,' Thomas said with a hint of judgment.

John scurried up the small ladder attached to the back of the church and climbed into the belfry. He grabbed a thick rope dangling from a large bell and pulled as hard as he could.

'Dong!...Dong!...Dong!' The sound rang out through all of Elstow and probably all the way to Bedford.

John was moving so fast that he almost fell trying to get down. They darted for his back door and stopped close enough to hear his father walk through the house and out of the front. They slipped in, wiped their faces of sweat and took off their outer shirts, tossing them into his room. They walked out the front door and stood with his father, trying to keep their breathing under control.

Mr Bunyan was looking down toward the church, scanning the street for any action. 'Ruffians!' He turned toward the boys. 'Thomas, I didn't know that you were over.'

'Yes, sir. Is that well with you?'

'It's fine. I'm just glad you two are here at home and not getting into trouble. Well, get some sleep.' He turned and walked back into the house.

John took a deep breath and looked at Thomas. 'Now that was close,' he whispered with a big smile. 'Let's go in.'

* * *

The following Sunday, John went to church with his father, his step-mother and his brother, William. Christopher Hall, the vicar of the Elstow church, had conformed partly to the desires of the Puritans and partly to the Church of England.

Elstow was clearly on the side of the Puritan Parliament and Hall followed their wishes. He preached against Sunday sports, dancing and ringing the church bells for pleasure. He even named his son Oliver after Oliver Cromwell.

John hated going to church, but there he was, reading the sermon title on a large piece of rough paper tacked to a wall inside the church: 'Put on the Full Armour of God.'

'Sounds more like, "Put me to Sleep,"' he thought to himself as they found their pew, which happened to be the second-to-last pew in the church.

Vicar Hall stood up for the service to begin and read out of Ephesians, chapter six—the part about putting on the armour of God. While he was reading, an elderly couple quietly walked in the door of the church and asked John and his family to scoot down the pew.

As John shuffled down, he ran his hand along a rough piece of wood on the underside of the pew and a splinter penetrated his finger. John immediately yelled out the Lord's name and the whole church stopped in silence.

All heads turned and the colour of John's face increased from one shade of red to the next. He had just blasphemed the holy name of God—and he knew it. He looked around the room at the silent crowd. Their eyes felt like a hundred little daggers pricking his damnable soul.

John's father took him by the collar, walked down the length of the pew and marched outside. 'I don't care who you think you are, but you are not going to embarrass me in church,' his father said, teeth clenched. 'After the service, we are going to talk with Vicar Hall about your punishment. Now go back inside and sit down.'

They sat back down, but John didn't listen to anything else the pastor said. His mind was racing. 'What is everybody's problem?' He felt like everyone was out to get him—just waiting for him to sin so they can throw stones. 'Besides, why did father have the right to call me out like that? He does the same thing at home when nobody's looking. I've seen him.'

After the service, people greeted the pastor as they walked out of the back door. John's step-mother and brother went home while he and his father remained, sitting in silence. Waiting for punishment almost seemed worse that the actual punishment itself.

After the people left, Vicar Hall came and sat on the other side of John. 'Do you know what you did?' asked the pastor in a low grisly voice.

John looked down. 'Yes sir. I broke the third commandment—I took the Lord's name in vain.'

'Is this a regular sin for you?' The pastor leaned over trying to look into John's eyes.

John paused. 'Sometimes. When I hit my finger in father's shop I have developed a habit of taking the Lord's name in vain—but it's always quiet.'

The pastor looked around as if he were examining the church building. Something outside must have caught his attention because he started staring out the window. 'The fence needs painting. Be here tomorrow afternoon ready to paint.'

'Could I not do it now and be done with it?' John blurted out.

The pastor peered at John in disgust. 'It's Sunday. I will see you tomorrow afternoon. You must pray for repentance tonight.'

'Pray for repentance?' John thought. Praying would have never crossed his mind, especially if he thought God was angry with him.

That night, he sat on his bed in his room. 'Pray for repentance.' The words kept churning in his mind. He knelt and bowed his head. 'Heavenly Father,' He paused and took a deep breath. 'Heavenly Father, I beseech…' Standing up he muttered 'I can't do this. How can I pray to a God I hardly believe in?'

All of the sudden—and to his amazement— a passage of Scripture came to his head. It was 1 Timothy 1:15, *'This is a faithful saying, and worthy of all acceptation, that Christ Jesus came into the world to save sinners, of whom I am chief.'* He remembered it from his childhood, when he sat through catechism classes at the Elstow church. By 1647, some people were using the King James Version authorized in 1611, but most were still using the Geneva Bible. All of the Scripture he learned growing up came from the 1599 edition of the Geneva Bible.

As he sat on his bed, lonely and depressed, he felt like he was the *'chief of sinners.'* 'Perhaps, though, I am not beyond the grace of God. Perhaps.' With slight comfort, he stretched out on his bed and fell asleep.

When John walked up to the front steps of the church the next day, Vicar Hall had already placed a brush and a bucket of white paint outside the door. The fence was in bad shape. 'It should have been painted a while ago,' he thought as he inspected the posts.

With brush in hand, he began on the side closest to the church building. His father could see him from down the road so there was no way of getting away with taking breaks. He actually didn't mind painting. In fact, it gave him some satisfaction when he looked back down the row of freshly-painted boards.

As he turned the corner to begin the side nearest the street, he saw a familiar carriage coming his way with a familiar tall, thin man on top. John quickly ran his fingers through his thick brown hair and stood up to address the visitor.

'Good day sir,' John called, waving his hands in the air.

'Wouuw,' the man said as his pulled the horse to a stop. 'Have we met young man?' he said, looking at John.

'No, sir. But I met your daughter briefly the other day in my father's shop.'

The man looked puzzled. 'Your father's shop?'

'Yes, I worked on your pots.'

'Ah, yes. They are splendid. Thank you Mr...'

'Bunyan, sir. John Bunyan.'

The man nodded. 'Thank you, John.'

Several long awkward seconds passed as John tried to peer into the carriage. 'Is your daughter with you?' John asked, looking back at the man.

'Hello John,' came a gentle voice followed by a face out of the side window of the carriage.

John gulped and quickly adjusted his trousers. 'Hello Mary.' She was even more beautiful than he remembered.

She glanced over to the freshly-painted fence. 'I see you are a man of many talents—first making pots, now painting a fence. You must love the Lord to be serving the church like that.'

John froze. He didn't want to tell her that this was his punishment for taking the Lord's name in vain, especially in front of her father. 'Yes, I do love the Lord and it is a great honour to serve His church by painting this fence,' he responded, putting his hands in his pockets.

Suddenly, he heard his father calling down the road. 'John, no breaks until you finish painting. Leave those people alone and get back to work!'

His pale face looked like it had just seen a ghost. 'Did that really just happen?' he thought to himself. He looked at Mary, but she gave him a frown and disappeared back into the carriage. Her father grabbed the reigns tightly. 'Heya!' he yelled as the horse jolted and started walking away.

'Wait!' yelled John, desperately trying to look into the carriage. 'I can explain. It's not what you think.' But it was too late. The carriage was not stopping nor turning back.

As the sun began to fade over the hills, so did any hope of seeing Mary. He picked up his brush and knelt back down next to the fence. 'I could have loved her,' he thought, shaking his head. 'Perhaps one day I will.'

Family Names and Sunday Games

Mary tip-toed along the back of the house, slightly lifting up her dress as she tried to avoid the mud. This was, after all, her only dress and she couldn't afford it getting dirty. A gust of cold air hit against the wood panelled wall and she felt her chapped lips with her tongue. Winters in Elstow were usually damp and the frigid temperature seemed unrelenting. She was now wishing she had taken her wool shawl along with her.

When she got to the side of the house, she peered around the corner to John's shop across the street, hoping nobody would see her trying to catch a glimpse of him.

'Where is he?' she thought to herself, scanning the surrounding area. She could see her breath vanishing into the cold air out in front of her. Just then, she heard a bang and a loud yelp. John raced out the door of the shop swatting at an array of bright-orange coals on his trousers.

Mary quickly stepped back behind the corner of the wall and giggled. Ever since her father died a few months earlier, John had been writing to her, trying to both comfort her and, quite boldly, win her affection. Nobody had ever written her like that before.

She slowly edged her head around the corner again when suddenly she heard her name being called in a loud voice.

'Mary?' a female voice exploded from the street.

Mary's heart began pounding in her head. 'It's mother,' she whispered to herself, quickly pulling her head back again from around the corner of the house. 'Why is she looking for me over here?' Mary had told her mother that she was going to Gabriel Coffey's bakery for bread, which was three blocks south of John's house.

'Mary?' her mother called again. 'Excuse me, lad, have you seen a young lady about your age walking up this way?' Mary couldn't see who she was talking to, but she knew it was John. 'She has a homely disposition and is quite shy, but I believe she may have passed by here.'

Mary stiffened and her eyes widened.

'No ma'am,' John answered. 'I have not seen such a lady, but did you say her name was Mary?'

'What do I do?' Mary thought to herself.

'Yes, Mary is her name,' her mother replied with a suspecting voice.

Mary wouldn't let her mother ruin any chance she might have with John. Lifting her dress off the ground, she took a deep breath and walked around the corner of the house toward them.

'Mary?' the two of them said in union. They looked at each other in confusion.

Her mother glared back at Mary. 'What are you doing behind that house?'

'I was just....' Mary looked back to the house herself. 'Just walking a bit further, mother.' Her mother had always been protective—too protective in Mary's opinion.

Her mother turned to John. 'And who are you and how do you know my daughter?'

'My name is John Bunyan, ma'am,' he said, still brushing a few remaining coals from his breeches' leg. He glanced over at Mary with a half-smile. 'I have been writing your daughter for a few months now trying to—'

'He's an honest man, mother,' Mary piped in. She pointed to John's house. 'He works as a tinker here in his father's shop.'

Her mother seemed to actually be more interested in John and, surprisingly, less worried about why Mary was so far from the bakery. 'So are the two of you...' She paused. 'Courting each other?'

Mary looked at John as if he were to define their relationship right then and there. John felt like his whole body went numb.

The small wedding took place outside of the west boundary of Elstow in a rather unknown country church. Though it was a joyful occasion, the death of Mary's father was present on everybody's mind. After the wedding, John and Mary settled into a small cottage near his father's house, though he continued to work from his father's shop to support himself and his new bride.

Mary's family was very poor. In fact, the only things her father left her when he passed away were two books—*The Plain Man's Pathway to Heaven* by Arthur Dent and *The Practice of Piety* by Lewis Bayly.

Bunyan liked to read on occasion, mostly fables and current news. He had read parts of the Bible when he was younger, but had never picked up what his father called, 'books for the soul.'

March of 1649 was unlike any other. The king of England, Charles I, was beheaded for high treason less than two months prior on 30 January. After his execution, a new republic was declared, the 'Commonwealth of England.'

At that time, it seemed as though everybody rallied behind the Puritans and their cause against King Charles. Now there seemed to be a growing fear and insecurity among the people of foreign attack. Who were the people to look to for protection? Who would rise up to defend England from France or from the Catholic armies in Ireland? All eyes turned to the natural defender and military leader of the Civil War, Oliver Cromwell.

But even still, fear hung thick in the air. On the heels of war, the beheading of a king and the constant panic of the unknown, people everywhere began searching—searching for surety and steadfast hope.

They looked to the God who was constant and did not change—the God revealed in the Bible.

John found himself picking up the two books Mary brought with her into their home in Elstow. He would read them by their fireplace at night, after working in the shop.

'John, won't you come to bed?' Mary asked again, trying not to be a nuisance.

John didn't move. All you could hear was a slight mumble coming from his mouth. His eyes were glued to the book *The Practice of Piety*. It was almost as if he had hung a 'Do Not Disturb' sign on the back of his wooden chair. Mary smiled and quietly went to bed.

'Would You wash my sins and transgressions clean from me, with the virtue of that most precious blood, which Your Son Jesus Christ has shed for me.'

The words would not leave John's mind: 'wash my sins and transgressions clean from me.' For some reason, the message pleased him, but his heart didn't break. He wasn't convicted of sin like he knew he should be. He knew that he was a sinner—like everybody else—but it was like he didn't really care.

John closed the book and slouched a little in his chair. The fire was now only a bright-red heap of coals. 'I feel like I need to get my life cleaned up,' he thought to himself, looking back down at his book.

That Sunday, John and Mary went to the Elstow church to hear Vicar Hall. They didn't have much choice—it was against the law not to go and could result in fines, or worse. As they sat down, John remembered again the awful experience of yelling out the Lord's name in vain. 'I've been better in my language since then,' he thought to himself, cracking a confident smile.

As Vicar Hall began to preach, John found himself strangely enamoured and fascinated by the reverence and solemnity of the service. The altar, which had not been torn down by the Puritans, stood out more than usual as a sacred table. Strangely, too, the ceremonial vestments worn by Hall, the *Book of Common Prayer*, and even Vicar Hall himself began to take on a new clout and pomp that John had not felt before. What was it about the worship?

'You see, my friends,' Hall continued, 'there is no place for sin in your life. Hear this, the Word of the Lord from Colossians three, verse five:

'Mortify therefore your members which are upon the earth; fornication, uncleanness, inordinate affection, evil concupiscence, and covetousness, which is idolatry.'

Suddenly, John felt compelled to completely avoid sin and idolatry. He looked over at his father, who now sat a couple of pews in front of him and who seemed to be daydreaming. John stared down at the ground. 'Am I the only one who feels like this?' he thought to himself.

As Hall finished and the people started filing out of the church, John tried to suppress his feelings and quickly found Thomas Bray, who was also trying to find him.

'The usual?' Thomas asked smiling.

John quickly tried to glance down the street. 'I'll see you there!'

Men usually worked six days a week. Although many observed the Sabbath day and rested, some had a hard time resting. John was in this latter group. As far as he was concerned, Sunday was his day, not the Lord's. He had worked hard all week and he wasn't going to let any of his ruffian friends get the better of him at tip-cat due to his lack of play.

Tip-cat was a game that involved a wooden block (the 'cat') about three or four inches long, tapered at the ends, and a stick—used as a bat—three feet long. With the stick, someone would strike one end of the 'cat' into the air (tipping the cat), and then swing at it. Points would be tallied according to the number that comes up on the four-sided cat, and then running from base to base on a large circle while the cat is retrieved.

John seemed to have a particular knack for the game and he tried not to let others forget that either.

John and some of the other men would meet on the village green to play. It was almost an open rebellion to the Puritans' 'no recreation' laws of 1644. Although the laws were not enforced in Elstow in 1649, they were certainly tabooed by the 'godly,' as they called themselves.

A 'Puritan' was one who initially reacted against the 'compromise' of the Elizabethan Settlement (1559) in favour of a more thorough reformation in England; who, socially, promoted evangelism, catechism, and spiritual nourishment through the preaching and teaching of the Bible; who, theologically, followed in the footsteps of John Calvin[*] and who strove for personal holiness, a practical faith and communion with God.

Keeping the Sabbath was clearly part of keeping God's law and vitally important for a person's spiritual growth. But at the moment, John was interested in trying to round the bases.

'Grab that cat!' yelled a short middle-aged man who was going bald. But John had already made it around the bases.

Out of breath, John glanced over to some of the 'godly' going to their homes for afternoon catechism. He had heard about the new confession of faith and catechisms that had just been written two years prior in 1647—the Westminster Confession of Faith and the Larger and Shorter Catechisms. Though the Westminster Assembly was heavily puritanical, Vicar Hall—himself part of the Church of England—would cite many of its doctrinal statements.

John watched the doors of the houses close and then bent over, still a bit out of breath. There was something appealing about catechism—the series of question and answer instruction about the Christian faith.

60   [*] Have you read the trailblazer on John Calvin? *After Darkness Light*

He frowned. 'Am I breaking God's Sabbath by playing tip-cat?'

He immediately felt as though Jesus himself was saying to him, 'Will you leave your sins and go to heaven, or have your sins and go to hell?' A shiver shot down his spine and he stood up, trying to shake it off. He felt like he was experiencing God's displeasure then and there.

Then he thought about Mary who was already home setting out food for lunch. His father and step-mother were probably doing their own part of Sabbath-keeping by now—sleeping.

John suddenly felt a hard slap on his back, half-way knocking the remaining wind out of his lungs. He whirled around and saw Thomas smiling back at him. 'It's your turn to catch,' Thomas said as if he was personally challenging John.

John looked down the street toward his home. 'I think I need to go home, my friend. Mary's waiting.'

The next morning, John got up early to work in the shop. The sun had just begun to rise over the hills on the east side of Elstow and the crisp morning air refreshed John's spirit. It was almost as if God were giving him a new start on life, or maybe just a new appreciation for the 'things of God.'

The first task written on the sheet next to the furnace was Ms Hamilton's kettle. He looked down at the broken top lying next to the kettle and then back at the sheet. 'I'll save that for father,' he thought to himself using his finger to scan down the other items on the list.

'Ah-ha! Another sword. This one is for Mr... Dentici?' he said, questioning his pronunciation. He was one of the few customers John hadn't met before. 'An Italian?' he thought as he tried to say it again in a slightly different way.

He looked around for the sword, but didn't see it. He noticed the dark furnace. 'First things first.'

He grabbed some cotton and a piece of flint hanging by a string next to the furnace and began stacking some small kindling around the cotton. After a few strikes, the cotton was ablaze. Most of the time, fires for the rest of the week didn't require the flint since there were usually a few hot coals left over from the previous night. A few pieces of cotton and some steady blowing would do it.

After stoking the fire and watching it consume some oak logs he had pulled from a nearby bin, he sat down on a stool between the anvil and the water trough. There was something about watching a fire that sent his mind chasing after deeper subjects.

He thought about playing tip-cat the day before and a sense of guilt slowly invaded his conscience. There was no way around it. The fourth commandment was becoming clearer by the minute: *'Remember the Sabbath day, to keep it holy.'* The words hung on John's mind like the anvil sitting beside him.

Before he knew it, he was running down the street toward the church. When he arrived, he walked in through the white fence—surveying his paint job—to the front door. He knew that Vicar Hall wouldn't be there yet, but he walked in anyhow.

The wood timbers creaked under his feet as he made his way down the middle aisle. His fingers felt the sides of the wooden pews, paying attention to the well-worn edges from many years of use.

The Elstow church was originally an Abby used by Benedictine nuns. It was built in 1078 by the niece of William I, Judith of Lens, and dedicated to St Mary. After Henry VIII's break with the Roman Catholic Church in 1534, it went into dissolution. The nuns were given a pension and left. The people of Elstow, however, continued to use the building for a church.

The faint beams of light coming in through the stained glass illuminated the baptismal font on the west end of the church. On the east end of the church stood the altar, which had been railed off in the late 1630s under Archbishop William Laud.

The 'altar' had become a central point of controversy during the 1630s and 40s. Archbishop Laud believed the Lord's Supper to be the 'high point' in the worship service, even greater than the sermon because that was—according to Laud—the greatest place of God's residence on earth. But naming it an 'altar,' having people kneel when they partook of the bread and wine (as a sign of worship), and railing it off showed all the elements of a Roman Catholic Mass. The Catholics believed that the bread and wine actually became the body and blood of Christ. Thus, when the elements were placed on the altar, Christ was sacrificed—every week.

In the 1640s, the Puritans had gone through many parts of England tearing down the railings and placing (as they called it) the Communion Table in the centre—allowing all to come and take the bread and wine. They believed that Christ was spiritually present in the bread and wine, not his actual body. As far as they were concerned, Christ died once for all (Hebrews 10:10).

For some reason, the Puritans had not torn down the railings at the Elstow church, but left it at the east end and railed off. John walked within a few feet of it and stopped, inspecting the table. 'Was this really the greatest place of God's residence on earth?' he thought to himself.

He wanted to touch it, but partially out of fear, decided not to. All of the sudden, he felt he was standing on holy ground. The chancel, the nave, the baptismal font and the altar all seemed to shout 'holy, holy, holy' like he had not experienced before.

Just then, he heard the side door's latch open and hinges creak. It was Vicar Hall. He immediately saw John standing beside the altar. 'John?

'Yes, sir. I have come to...,' John said, pausing and looking back at the altar. 'I have come to pray. Is that alright?'

'Of course. But I am surprised to see you here, especially so early in the morning. Is there something you wish to talk about?'

By this point, John was wondering why he had ever come in the first place. 'Well, I did have one question.'

'Go on,' Hall said slowly walking over toward the altar.

'Is God angry with me? You see, I have broken the Lord's Sabbath by playing games—for most of my life!' The more he talked, the louder he became. 'And I feel that God has in store for me great judgment and wrath!'

Hall, by this point, stood only several feet from John and was leaning on the side of one of the pews. 'If you accept Christ and trust in his sacrifice on the cross to save you then as our Lord has said, from the top of that dreadful cross, "It is finished." Trust in his work on your behalf, John, and you will never taste God's judgment.'

Hall's tone and answer seemed to convey great truth, but John felt that his heart was still cold to such a gospel. He felt guilt, but no grace.

'Do you have a Bible that I may borrow?' John asked. After leaving his father's house, he could not afford a Bible of his own.

'Of course, but you may only read it here in the church.' He pointed over to a book chained to a table below one of the windows. 'It mustn't leave the property.'

The experience in the church that day made his appetite for the holy insatiable. He knew that there was something deeper than the rituals and the objects used in worship, but he didn't understand it or believe it.

As 1649 came to an end and a new year dawned, Mary became pregnant with their first child, named after her mother. But after some time they discovered that she was blind. It was a hardship and they knew that it would end up being a hard life for their little one too.

Over the next eight years, the Bunyan's would have three more children. But the birth of Mary, their first, made a lasting mark on John's still impressionable soul. It was hard for him to reconcile God's goodness and power together with suffering and evil.

Nevertheless, John and Mary continued to worship at the Elstow church and John would even go twice a day to talk with Vicar Hall or simply to admire the presence of the holy. But in 1652, that all changed.

Thank you John Gifford!

Even though the trees still looked dead and bare, John could feel the excitement of the approaching spring. He walked at a brisk pace, trying to make it to Bedford early enough to catch people as they made it out of their homes for work, school or starting their daily chores.

The morning air was still quite cold, but the sun's glow that spread across the fields somehow warmed his soul. If it were not for the constant banging of pots and pans, one against the other, he would probably really enjoy the two-mile trek.

The wooden cart had two wheels toward the front and a pole sticking down in the rear. When lifted, the cart rolled with ease except when John would hit a rock or a divot in the road.

A rather short stone wall ran along to his right that held sheep. John looked over and remembered a passage of Scripture he had read the week before from John, chapter 10, where Jesus said: *'I am the good shepherd: the good shepherd giveth his life for the sheep.'*

He immediately started thinking about how much his life had changed over the last few months. 'I have put bell-ringing, dancing and even sports on Sunday in the past,' he thought to himself still glancing over at the sheep.

Not only had John quit doing these things, he had also started having theological discussions with Vicar Hall on a regular basis—so much so that he had learned quite a bit of theology and church history.

At first, he was truly curious and interested in learning about God and the Bible, but as time went on, he started learning those things just to impress his neighbours at church on Sunday. And sure enough, they were all shocked by the change—'the town clown turns to Jesus'—seemed to be the appropriate headline.

As John made it to the bridge looking over the Great Ouse River, he could see more and more people walking, riding horses or greeting each other from their front doors.

The river looked calm and peaceful. 'That would be a cold swim,' he thought, giving a small chuckle. At the top of the bridge, he stopped and saw two men in a long, skinny wooden boat trolling a fishing net and John wished he had brought his pole.

They were tying rocks to the sides of a net and pieces of wood to the middle. When they dropped the net in the water, the sides quickly sank to the bottom while the centre stayed at the top. After a minute or two, they would grab the floating wood and pull the net into the boat along with the trapped fish.

Just watching them was like being caught in their net. John looked on, anticipating how many fish they could bring up each time, as if it were a competition with each cast of the net.

'Get moving, lad!' suddenly barked a rough baritone voice.

John whirled around and saw a familiar man with a bushy brown beard and dirty hands trudging by.

'I wonder if he knows anything of religion,' John thought frowning. He wondered if the man was a reprobate—someone whom God chooses for damnation. John was fairly confident that he was one of God's elect. How could he not be? If God knows all, he certainly knew how much time John had spent in church reading the Bible and talking with Vicar Hall.

By this point, the sun was hitting the entire east side of St Paul's church. He rolled the cart to 'his' corner of the square and sat down on a wooden stool which he had fastened to the back of the cart.

As he sat with his back leaning against the cart and waited for a potential customer, he overheard some female voices talking from across the street. Four women were sitting on the front steps of a large brick building in the sun and looked to be sewing different parts of a quilt. He could tell that they were not wealthy from their clothing and from the fact that they were sitting on the steps—rich women didn't sit on steps.

'Was not Reverend Gifford extraordinary last Sunday?' a petite middle-aged lady said to the others. 'Oh, indeed. The Lord is so gracious and compassionate that he would even look upon us in love,' another responded. 'We are blessed to have such a gentle yet spiritual man be our shepherd.'

John immediately felt compelled to walk over and engage with them in conversation, especially since he knew a great deal of theology and Bible. But before he could stand up, he overheard something—something that forever changed his heart.

'I am so wretched,' one of the women said looking down as if she were about to cry. 'I have been outwardly professing the Christian religion, but in my heart, I am terribly sinful and prideful. I am honouring God with my lips, but my heart is far from him. I hate my sinful flesh!'

John didn't move.

She looked up at the rest of the women and then up toward the sky. 'Forgive me, Lord!' She burst out in uncontrollable tears and the other ladies moved closer and wrapped their arms around her.

All of a sudden, John felt a weight of conviction like an enormous boulder pressing against his heart. 'I am undone and broken,' he whispered to himself, his eyes fixated on what he had just witnessed. 'Her sin is my sin.'

That morning, witnessing the true conviction of a humble and broken woman, John looked up to the heavens and prayed. God had granted him a believing heart and he embraced Jesus Christ as his Saviour. The external religion that he had been wearing was broken and his soul was freed from the bonds of sin.

* * *

John's father walked out of the shop and looked at John. 'What have you for dinner?'

'The usual—a loaf and some eggs,' John said looking down at his meal.

John and his father had just finished hammering some plough wheels for a family in Bedford and were taking a break for lunch.

'I hear that you are going to Bedford this Lord's Day to hear John Gifford,' his father said sitting down on a bench in front of the shop.

'Yes, sir. He preaches at the Church of St John. I've been invited by some people I met last week in Bedford.' John wasn't sure what his father would think of him going to another town for worship.

'It's just for a visit, right?' his father questioned, peering at John.

John didn't know what else he could say. 'Just a visit.'

That Sunday, however, marked a turning point in John's life. For there in Bedford, he found a community of faith like he had never experienced at the Elstow church.

The Civil War that had taken place in the 1640s was started primarily over religious differences. The King desired a church government that sympathized with Roman Catholics while Parliament favoured a more puritanical Presbyterian and Congregationalist form of church government, which was ruled by the *people*, not the king. However, when it became clear that Cromwell and the Parliamentary army were in power by 1650, the Congregationalists became the dominant religious group.

When the fighting ceased, Congregationalism—which argued for individual disconnected churches ruled by the people—seemed to be a nice alternative to any type of church government that could potentially oppress the people from the top down.

Bedford fell right in the middle of this national conflict. As a minister of the national church and a Fellow of Emmanuel College, Cambridge, William Dell became enormously influential in Bedfordshire. Not only was he a chaplain in the Parliamentary army under General Fairfax and a Congregationalist at heart, he controlled the rectory in Bedfordshire, which greatly influenced church life in the town of Bedford.

In 1650, a church was founded upon the principles of a Congregational-style church government, which was ruled by the people of that congregation and not from any outside ruler or authority. This church would be the church Bunyan found himself attending in the late spring and early summer of 1652. The minister of this small congregation was John Gifford, who was probably the least likely candidate for the job.

At the outbreak of the Civil War, Gifford was a Royalist and a major in the King's army. In 1648, after it was clear that Charles was defeated, he helped start an uprising near Kent to win back the country for the king.

Some ten to twelve thousand men began marching toward London with drums and banners. At Rochester, they were met by Parliamentary forces under the Lord General Fairfax and the ensuing battle turned into one of the bloodiest and lowest points of the Civil War. With Fairfax taking the victory, some 1,400 Royalist soldiers were taken prisoner, including Gifford.

For taking a lead part in the uprising, Gifford was sentenced to be hanged. But the night before his execution, his sister visited him in his cell and encouraged him to escape. Later that night, when the guards were either drunk or had fallen asleep, he took his chance and passed through them all and ran into a nearby field.

A search went on for three days, but Gifford had hid in a ditch and covered himself with leaves. Disguised, he left London and travelled north to Bedford. He had some experience practising medicine before entering the Royalist army and so took on the profession of a doctor.

Quickly, however, he became known for much more than that. He had a drinking problem and would always go around swearing and gaming—until one night, while drunk, he picked up some Puritan literature and began reading. All of a sudden, the Lord changed his heart and he was convicted of sin. It wasn't for another month however that he grasped God's forgiveness in Christ Jesus and no sooner found himself in fellowship with other committed Christians.

The Lord pressed upon his heart that he should preach, though many doubted such a divine call. After preaching before a private audience in a home, word spread that he was gifted in this area and before long, he was asked to preach publicly.

After preaching in various places around Bedfordshire and having some acquaintance with other ministers, he took on the task of organizing a church of his own by talking to various men and women around the town.

After some time, twelve signed their names at the charter meeting in 1650 and formally accepted Gifford as their pastor. Significantly, one of these charter members was then the mayor of Bedford, John Easton.

Because the nation in general and Bedford in particular—thanks to William Dell—had swung toward Congregationalism, many welcomed the new 'hands-off' approach of Cromwell's early rule. After his rise to power, all that was required officially for a person to become a minister was for a group of 'responsible people' to testify to the character and gifts of a 'called' individual to the ministry. That was all. No articles of faith were prescribed (except that you couldn't be a Roman Catholic or a 'heretic') and no denomination was mentioned.

Cromwell's establishment recognized no one form of church organization. Therefore, under this system, there was nothing to prevent local Commissioners from admitting John Gifford to the rectory of the Hospital and Church of St John in Bedford.

'Flee your life of sin and run to Christ, who is your righteousness.' Gifford's words rang loud and clear in Bunyan's ears. St John's Church was not that unlike the church in Elstow. It had a long nave with wooden pews on each side of a central aisle. It was a little odd being in a different place of worship, but Gifford's preaching was bolder and more penetrating than that of Vicar Hall. Besides, Gifford had broken away from the established Church of England, unlike Hall.

As the service finished, he felt a tap on his shoulder. 'Pardon me, sir.'

John turned around.

'Are you Mr Bunyan?' asked an elderly fellow with red cheeks.

'Yes, I am,' John answered, wondering who he was.

The gentleman stood up with his hand extended. 'Delighted to meet you. I've heard that you have knowledge of theology and God's Holy Word.'

John didn't want to come across as arrogant, but he did know some theology. 'I have read a bit and enjoy conversation in the subject.'

'Very well.' The man pulled out an old book from under a copy of a new Bible, which John saw was the King James Version. 'I would like to give this to you,' the man said handing the book to John. 'It is a copy of Martin Luther's Commentary on Galatians.'

John took the book and looked back up at the gentleman. 'Thank you, sir.'

'I've had it for years and have been meaning to give it to a young chap who would appreciate it,' the man said smiling.

John certainly did appreciate it. Martin Luther had died in 1546, but he was still a symbol of freedom and truth. He helped 'free' the church from the bonds of Roman Catholic rituals and empty worship and had opened up the Bible for his native countrymen in the German language.

John felt the rough leather binding in his hands and looked to see the publishing date, but that page was missing. Before he knew what was happening, the man had walked down the pew and out of the church.

'Martin Luther,' he said quietly to himself, opening up to the Preface again.

As he walked out, he thanked Gifford. 'Thank you, John Gifford. God's Word has gone forth and has returned with much fruit.' And John meant every word of it.

Over the next year, John studied, dissected and laboured with Luther on the doctrines of grace and justification by faith alone. Next to the Bible, this book became John's constant companion. The combined team of Gifford and Luther mentored the twenty-four year old tinker from Elstow and the Spirit of God continued to sanctify his heart.

After several months of attending Gifford's church, he was asked to become a member, to fully give himself to the overall mission and vision of the church and to be under the discipline of a body of believers. In 1653, he did just that. He joined the Bedford church.

No longer did he make the two-mile journey to Bedford just to sell various metal wares, he also would stop to talk with Gifford or some of the other members of the small, but growing community of faith. Their zeal for the Lord inspired him to examine his own heart for evidence of sin and also for God's power at work in his life.

Though excitement surrounded the new church, John still had troubles at home. The constant pressures of work, the stress of providing for his family and raising a blind child took its toll on him. He spent many hours pouring his heart out to God.

But that wasn't all he had going on. During the autumn of 1653, Mary became pregnant with their second child.

During the 1650s, giving birth was very dangerous. Many babies—and mothers—died due to a lack of knowledge, unsuitable conditions or other complications with the delivery. A woman would usually deliver her child at home with the help of a midwife.

When it came to the time for the baby to be born John wasn't allowed in the room or in the house. Actually, no male was allowed near the delivery room at all. He paced outside with his father waiting for the first sound of the baby's crying. At the moment, however, all he could hear was Mary's yelling.

'God, please protect my wife and child,' he whispered to himself. He knew the risks involved from hearing about many, even in Elstow, who had died from childbirth.

'It will be alright, my son,' his father said placing his hand on John's shoulder. 'God is in control, even now.' It was strange how hearing somebody say something you already believed made that truth much more real and comforting. It was also strange how it was during the hard times that the people you least expected to say something like that were actually the first to say it.

But God was pleased to bless John and Mary with another baby girl in April 1654 and they named her Elizabeth—a strong Protestant name, full of symbolic meaning: strong, courageous, faithful and wise.

During the following months, his new friends from the church in Bedford supported him and his family and something struck him that he had never considered much before. These people served one another—they gave of themselves for other people selflessly. He was almost starting to feel closer to the people in Bedford than he was to the people in Elstow.

Every now and then, he saw people from the Elstow church stopping by the shop. They would ask him why he had been going to Bedford and quit going to hear Vicar Hall. The only answer he could give was that the Lord was working mightily in the ministry of John Gifford. There, too, in Bedford he felt that he had a fresh start. Not as many people knew him—or 'of him'—there.

To John's surprise, Gifford took a particular note of the spiritual depth of young Bunyan. John's life was about to take a drastic turn—more than he realized. The approaching danger was mysteriously tied to what would become his greatest delight—preaching God's Word.

Preach the Word!

John, Mary and their two girls huddled around the fire trying to stay warm. The dark night was met by an even darker fear of the unknown.

'I don't want to move, John,' Mary said, nervously stroking Elizabeth's hair. 'We have a home here in Elstow, two children and you have work.' Tears were beginning to well up in her eyes.

John was trying to be patient. 'But I feel that the Lord's place for us is in Bedford, with the ministry of John Gifford. Besides, work is slow now and there is more opportunity there.'

They all gazed at the leaping flames. The blistering cold was creeping in through the cracks around the door and, even though they had blankets over them while they sat facing the fire, the evening chill went to their bones. Next to the fireplace hung socks and wool jackets, which were steadily giving off steam from being damp all day.

John sat up in his chair and looked over at Mary. 'We must seek the Lord in this move and trust that He would prepare the way before us. The church in Bedford needs our help and it is becoming increasingly difficult to live two lives—one here and another there.'

Mary leaned over and kissed Elizabeth's head. 'I trust you, John. I'm just scared.'

The winter of 1655 was long and cold. There seemed to be much more time to think and even doubt God's continuing presence and less time outside—playing or working.

Through some contacts John had made at the new church, he was able to sell their home in Elstow and buy a small cottage on the outskirts of Bedford. Though only two miles away, moving was not easy. John had the task of going through all of the tools at his father's shop and picking out which ones he had purchased over the years to take with him. Their new cottage in Bedford would take some work, but John was ready for the challenge.

In the spring, the Bunyan family moved from Elstow and officially became residents of the town of Bedford. Ironically, the move symbolized much more than just a relocation—it symbolized a break from a life of unbelief and notorious sin.

Bedford was one of the most ancient boroughs in England, chartered during the reign of Henry II (1154–89). A charter of a town consisted of appointing a mayor, councillors, a recorder, a town clerk, field-drivers, bucket-keepers, ale-tasters, fishermen and wood-searchers.

When the Bunyans moved, Bedford's population was between one and two thousand people. The borough consisted of the same five parishes as at present, but the houses were—at that time—widely scattered, many of them having large fenced-in fields and orchards. The streets in town were lined with butcheries and fish shops, sheep-shearers and gun-makers. Of course, there were the ale-houses and sporting greens scattered throughout as well.

Most people in Bedford favoured the 'free republic' under Oliver Cromwell. William Dell, who controlled the rectory in Bedfordshire and was a Fellow at Emmanuel College, Cambridge, strongly opposed the monarchy. Such opposition influenced public opinion in Bedford and most were not afraid to express their feelings openly, especially in the ale-houses.

After the Bunyans moved, John began spending much more time with Rev Gifford and the people of the church in Bedford. But to John's surprise, God had greater plans in store for the young tinker.

'John, would you say a few words of exhortation before we begin our time of prayer and fasting,' one of the older men asked him. They were in the home of Mr and Mrs Harrington, a charter family of the Bedford church, and were praying that God would grant them fruitful labour for their work in ministry.

'I would not mind at all, my friend,' John said, feeling a lump in his throat. Standing up from his chair and opening a Bible, he addressed the small group assembled. 'From the second chapter of St Paul's epistle to the Ephesians, verse ten reads: *'For we are his workmanship, created in Christ Jesus unto good works, which God hath before ordained that we should walk in them.'* He read from a new copy of the King James Version, which was just now becoming more popular among the people—even though it was written in 1611.

'As we consider the work that lay before us in gospel ministry,' John began, while glancing around the room, *'we must note that the work is first and foremost God's work that he has ordained. In the second place, St Paul gives us a reason for which we were created—for 'good works.' We were created to plant and to water the gospel into the lives of people, but it is God who grants saving faith to the unbeliever.'* John spoke with urgency and conviction. His words carried a sense of authority and unwavering truth.

When he had finished, the room was in a state of shock—both from his unknown gifting as an expositor of God's Word, but also from God himself working in their hearts.

Over the next few months, John frequently addressed small gatherings of Christians, encouraging them from God's Word and explaining the truths found therein. Increasingly, he felt God's call on his life to leave his trade as a tinker and enter into full-time ministry. This was only confirmed by witnessing people's lives transformed under his teaching. But beginning in the late spring of 1655, John became deathly ill—suffering from fever, weakness and vomiting.

As Mary continued to wipe the sweat from his brow, John occasionally turned over the side of the bed, vomiting into a metal bucket. He couldn't keep anything down. John Gifford, himself a physician, frequently stopped by the Bunyan's cottage to check in and pray.

'Lord God, we beseech Thee to rid John of this attack and illness for your glory. May he find rest in Thee even now, we pray.' Despite the prayers and visits, John's condition continued to get worse. And there, in the midst of it all, he felt Satan's attack upon his faith more than ever.

'Away from me!' John pleaded, grimacing in pain. 'Away from me, you worker of evil!' He pictured an overwhelming dragon hurling arrows at him and asking him to renounce his faith in Christ. 'I am a son of the living God and you have no power over me!' he yelled. Then he remembered a sermon that Vicar Hall had preached from Ephesians, chapter 6 about putting on the 'armour of God.' In it, Paul talked of the 'sword of the spirit, which is the Word of God.' From the sermon, he had learned that the translation for 'Word' was literally the spoken word—as in speaking God's Word as a form of defense.

Immediately, John began quoting Scripture to counter-attack Satan's bidding. Over time, he felt relief from the Tempter's attacks and found strength in God. He even began feeling well enough to attend church on occasion.

* * *

The summer of 1655 was busier than ever. Not only had Mary given birth to a third child—a son—but the people at the church nominated John to be a deacon, which was an official office of the church designated for service. All believers in Christ were called to serve, but a deacon was to lead the way by example and personal piety.

Having seen John's faith in action and even under attack by Satan, the people at St John's church were overwhelmingly in support of the decision.

As John knelt before the congregation, Gifford placed his hands on John's shoulders and addressed all who were present. 'By order of God's Holy Word, for the peace and purity of Christ's church and for the ministry to those who are in need, to the sick, to the friendless and to any who may be in distress, we ordain you, John Bunyan, to the office of deacon. May God grant you a faithful heart and fruitful ministry. Amen.'

John suddenly felt that he had been set apart for a holy calling. Even so, he didn't feel adequate. He still struggled with sin and temptation. But greater still, he felt that he was clothed in the righteousness of Christ, his Lord.

John stood up and faced the congregation, who all added their 'Amen' to Gifford's pronouncement. He looked back at Gifford in both awe and gratitude. Here was a man who once fought with King Charles, who lived a life of drunkenness and debauchery and who now stood as the pastor of this growing flock in Bedford.

Gifford was God's gift to Bunyan. John had never learned more about Scripture or what a lived-out faith looked like than from this pastor of God, John Gifford.

But to everyone's shock, Gifford died suddenly and without warning in September of 1655. The sickness that came on one day, by the next morning, stole his last breath. The questions of 'why' again crept back into John's mind and heart—reminding him of so much tragedy in his own short life.

The abruptness of his death sent the congregation scrambling, trying to figure out who would replace such a man of God. But the town legislators had already chosen the man whom they wanted. The Common Council of Bedford released a statement on 19 September 1655 to announce John Gifford's replacement: Mr Hayes of Papworth.

But to the members of the church itself, this appointment was unwelcome and resisted. Certain men of the congregation drew up a written appeal, which made its way to the top, to Oliver Cromwell himself.

As many as six men appeared as agents on behalf of the church before Cromwell during the autumn of 1655. After much deliberation and argument, they won the case and immediately elected—with Cromwell's approval—Mr John Burton to replace Gifford as their new pastor. That winter, Whitehall issued a declaration:

Mr John Burton is by His Highness, Oliver, Lord Protector of England, under his seal manuall, nominated thereunto, the Commissioners for approbation of Publique Preachers having received a Testimony of the holy and good conversation of the said John Burton, and finding him to be a person qualified as in and by the Ordinance for such approbation is required, Doe by these present retifie, confirm, and allow the said John Burton to be and continue in the Hospitall aforesaid a Publique Preacher there.

John Burton, then, succeeded Gifford as the pastor of St John's Church in Bedford. However, under the strain of public life, Burton had delicate health and the weekly tasks and labours of ministry proved too hard for the young pastor. Despite his chronic illness, the people seemed to welcome and admire him.

But as time went on, the people knew they needed to have somebody ready to step in at a moment's notice, to preach God's word and to minister to the flock when Burton fell sick. It was then that the congregation in Bedford set apart John Bunyan as a Preacher of the Gospel and a Minister of Christ's church. When Burton could not preach, John rose to the occasion.

It was during this time, in the early months of 1656, that people began recognizing John's gifting as a preacher. Sometimes there would be weeks on end when Burton could not be there due to illness and John would step into the pulpit to proclaim God's Word.

'Christ Jesus is the truer and better David,' he told the congregation, preaching from 1 Samuel 17. 'It is not that we must face our giants, like David faced the giant Goliath. Christ has faced the giants for us, on our behalf. And now, we trust in his victory.'

The people didn't even blink.

'In fact, dear friends, you do not even have the ability to face your giants in life. That is the gospel—that you can't do it! Christ did—in his life—what you could never do in yours. And he died the death that you deserve.'

When he had finished, some were in tears and others began whispering words of amazement to one another. 'My, how he handles the Holy Scriptures,' one man said to another, leaning forward over the pew.

The press published literature about Bunyan and made its way around the countryside. Over the next few weeks, people from all over began coming to hear the new-found preacher of Bedford and marvel at the work God was doing in their midst. Popularity soon attached itself to Bunyan's name and news of his sermons made headlines.

But with popularity came attack. The doctors of the universities and the priests of the Church of England soon rose up to challenge his bold preaching. 'How could this tinker from the little town of Elstow become a learned expositor of God's Holy Word?' they asked themselves. 'He has not even been to university to learn doctrine or church government.'

The priests of the Church of England rallied against him hardest. Not only was he considered 'outside' the established Church of England with no education past grammar school, Bunyan emphasized the importance of the preached Word over the sacraments, especially the Eucharist. To many of the priests, this was an abomination. They believed the Lord's Supper to be highest point in the worship service and the place where Christ was most present.

But all of these criticisms didn't stop John from proclaiming the truths of Scripture on the weeks Burton was ill.

By the late spring of 1656, the flowers were in full bloom and John was trying to meet the demands of ministry on top of his work as a tinker. As time passed, he found himself spending much more time serving the people of the church and less time catching up on projects in his shop.

To begin with, he had not gotten off to a great start in Bedford. When he arrived, he spent so much time in the church that he wasn't able to find much business for his trade. Mary, of course, had a hard time letting John forget that. But slowly, over time, he had built up a small but regular flow of customers.

One hot afternoon, while working in the shop, he started thinking about Gifford. He missed his pastor and friend. It was because of Gifford's ministry that he and his family had moved to Bedford in the first place.

Sparks flew across the room as John pounded a metal wash basin that had been dented by a son who was quite often beaten by his parents. As John worked, he felt bad for the boy and wondered if he should have a talk with the parents.

'Who teaches a boy to rebel against his parents or parents to beat their children?' he thought to himself, sticking the basin back into a heap of burning coals.

'It's sin!' He already knew the answer, but it was really amazing how much of his experience with everyday life matched that reality found in Scripture.

The humid air hung thick that afternoon and sweat was pouring down his face and running into his eyes. 'Ouch,' he whispered to himself, trying to wipe the salty sweat from his face on his shirtsleeve.

As he began pounding the metal again, he heard a knock on the open door. 'Mr Bunyan?'

John turned around. 'Ah, Mr Harrington. Are you well, this day? How is your soul?'

The man paused. 'Fine.'

John put down his hammer and stood up. 'Come in,' he said motioning with his hand.

Mr Harrington walked in and sat down on a large oak log that John hadn't chopped yet. 'A hot day,' he said, taking off his periwig. It was becoming increasingly fashionable for men to shave their heads and wear a wig. In fact, it was a safety measure against lice, which would thrive in natural hair.

'Indeed it is,' John responded. John was beginning to think that Mr Harrington was not being totally direct or that something was weighing heavy on his mind. 'What's on your mind, my friend?'

'You see,' he started. 'I…I've sinned against my wife and children. I seem to have a problem with anger and fits of rage and I am not sure what to do.'

John could tell that the man really did feel a weight of guilt upon him. 'What kind of things bring about such anger?'

'Small things—my wife's food not tasting great or my children talking too loud. It's shameful and I feel that the Devil is dividing our home.'

John took a deep breath and peered into the man's eyes. 'May I give you words of advice?' he started.

'Yes, please.'

'First, confess your sin to your family and ask them to forgive you. The book of James, chapter five, exhorts us to confess our sin, one to another.'

Mr Harrington looked down at his boots, squirming a little, and then back up at John.

'Second, you are not only completely forgiven by Christ Jesus for your sin, you are also completely found righteous in the sight of God Almighty.'

The news seemed to shock Mr Harrington a little. 'I am righteous?' he asked with a puzzled look.

'Indeed, my friend. You are completely clothed in the righteousness of Christ. Your sin has been reckoned to him and his righteousness has been reckoned to you. Therefore, be free from your weight of guilt!' John spoke with a sincerity that Mr Harrington didn't expect.

The man stood up as did John. 'Thank you. Thank you, John, for your words.' And with that, Mr Harrington put on his periwig and walked out of the shop.

John sat back down. He felt both burdened by the man's problem and encouraged that the Lord had used him to minister to the fellow.

He turned around, sat down and picked up his hammer again. 'Thank you, Lord.' And with that, he went back to work.

Ink, Paper and the Quakers

John couldn't believe what he was hearing. A tall, dark-haired woman was standing at the Market Cross in Bedford, addressing a rapidly-growing crowd. 'Throw away the Scriptures and find the inner light offered by Christ.'

'Blasphemy!' yelled a middle-aged man, throwing his fist into the air. A general murmur spread among the people who had gathered and John could tell that he was in good company.

Suddenly, another came to her defense. 'My friends, she is right,' a young teenager said, finding a nearby stool to stand on. 'Why do you think the Civil War began?' He paused, as if he really did want somebody to answer him. 'The Civil War was brought about by differing interpretations of Scripture. It is Scripture that has divided us. God is in everyone and Christ teaches people himself—apart from the Bible.'

At this, some of the people yelled louder and threatened them with the gallows. 'You shall be hanged!'

But the two quickly started walking away down the street and disappeared behind a large house. Although the crowd stayed put, they continued to throw out curses upon what they had just heard.

The two represented a growing religious off-shoot sect of Christianity, called the Society of Friends, though most people knew them as the 'Quakers.' George Fox, their leader, believed that all men were born with a light within them which would lead and guide them. This 'inner light' was more reliable than any other guide—be it the Bible, the clergy, the church or the sacraments.

Quakerism, which began in 1648, had mushroomed to nearly 20,000 members by 1656. Although the sect never amounted to more than two percent of the entire population in England, they posed a serious danger in the eyes of many who were committed to finishing the Reformation in England.

The Protestant Reformers and the Puritans in England held firm to the idea that Scripture alone was the true authority for all faith and practice both in the church and in the world. The Quakers directly opposed this teaching and maintained that God still reveals his will, even if it is contrary to what the Bible says. Therefore, anybody of any age could argue against Scripture solely based on what he or she believed to be revealed by the Spirit.

John had heard of the Quakers, but had not come into direct contact with any—until now. He figured that it was a fast-growing fad that would soon either be unpopular or be squelched by the authorities. But as the summer of 1656 drew to an end, Bunyan realized that he must fight the Quakers' influence himself—a move that thrust him to the centre stage in a national drama.

John stepped into the pulpit at St John's Church and opened his Bible. The place was packed. There were people there from as far as London waiting to hear the preacher of the hour. Undoubtedly, some were there because they didn't believe what they had heard— Elstow's uneducated tinker has become Bedford's prized preacher. Others, however, had come out of a sincere desire to hear God's Word expounded and taught.

'Deceived men are attacking our Lord Jesus Christ and his church,' John began, earnestly looking over the crowd. 'They insist that our Lord was not fully human, but rather his body only exists now spiritually in the form of the church.'

A slight stir moved through the people followed by some whispering.

'They insist that there is no place for the sacraments, no place for the great creeds and confessions and no place for God's Holy Word! They boast that their revelations are greater than the Bible.'

At this, the whispers became audible voices and even some bursts of opposition.

'But the first chapter of the Gospel of John states that "The Word was made flesh and dwelt among us, and we beheld his glory, the glory as of the only begotten of the Father, full of grace and truth." Our Lord is fully God and fully man! He was truly born into the world, truly died, truly buried, truly resurrected and most truly ascended to the right hand of the Father.'

'Hear, hear!' responded a majority of the congregation.

As John continued to preach, the people grew louder and louder until—

'Bang, bang, bang.' Everyone froze and turned, looking at the door. Suddenly, the door opened and a small mob of angry people entered into the nave.

'Away with the church!' one of them shouted. 'Away with the church!'

The whole congregation seemed to gasp at once.

John leaned over the pulpit and addressed the unwelcome visitors. 'Who are you and what right do you have to barge into God's house this Lord's Day?'

A tall dark-haired woman stepped forward, the same woman who had stirred up the crowed at the Market Cross a month earlier. 'My name is Anne Blackley and we are the Society of Friends. This service is an abomination to the Lord!'

The people were shocked.

'You are deceived!' John responded. 'The Bible says that we are to worship the Lord our God in spirit and in truth and that is what we are doing here today. The Bible is the scaffold* built by God on which the hope of sinners finds rest.'

---

* A foundation or framework like scaffolding round a building.

'Your Bible is an idol made with hands!' Anne shot back. 'Turn to the inner light—that is your only guide.'

Before John could say anything, she turned around and walked back out the door, followed by the others. John knew that he now stood in the spotlight. What was he to do?

It was not uncommon after a worship service that people stay and, publicly, ask the preacher questions or dispute a point he had made during the sermon. This day, however, John knew that he would have to do more than simply answer a few spoken questions; he would have to make a full-forced argument in writing.

That autumn, John spent much of his time at home, writing page after page of his thoughts and his exposition of the Scriptures concerning the person and work of Jesus Christ. He was writing what would become his first book, entitled *Some Gospel Truths Opened*. The book protested against the teachings of the Quakers and even called for their repentance and faith.

John Burton, the pastor then at St John's Church wrote the Preface, noting that he himself had experienced, with many others, Bunyan's soundness in the faith, his godly conversation and his ability to preach the gospel. The book—printed in London— would introduce young Bunyan to an even wider audience than his preaching.

But fame brought criticism. During the winter of 1657, *Some Gospel Truths Opened* fell into the hands of a certain man named Edward Burrough, a twenty-three year-old Quaker. Burrough quickly responded with his own treatise entitled *The True Faith of the Gospel of Peace* and, within two weeks, Bunyan counter-attacked with *A Vindication of Some Gospel Truths Opened*.

Although many were impressed by the wit and the theological power of Bunyan's mind, they were equally impressed by his style and use of the English language.

Out of the grim realities of war, attacks on God's Word and heated debates with the Quakers, a writer was born. Eventually writing over sixty works, Bunyan soon became known as much—if not more—for his writing than for his preaching. But the appearance of his books didn't slow the demand for his preaching.

From Cambridge to Coventry, from Northampton to London, pastors opened their pulpits to John. He preached in barns, village greens and homes. It was not uncommon to find him preaching on Sundays and then to hear of him preaching the following Tuesday or Friday. Where there were people, John preached the Word.

What exactly did 'preaching the Word' mean? During the mid-seventeenth century, pastors—who were Puritans like Bunyan—generally followed the same sermon structure. First, the minister would read a text from Scripture. Second, he would give a brief synopsis of the doctrines taught therein. Third, he would consider the context of the passage, collate other related passages and give the reasons for supporting such doctrines. Finally, the minister would apply the doctrines to the lives and experiences of the people in plain terms.

Bunyan's sermons generally followed this pattern throughout. Though preaching became the passion of his life, it was never easy for him. Sometimes he would be seized with a strange weakness of body on his way to where he would preach and then be tempted with the sin of pride at his hold and sway over those that listened.

Sometimes, when he thought that he had done no good in the pulpit, many were converted and many others greatly encouraged by the gospel. Other times, when he thought the sermon was going well, there seemed to be no real effect upon the listeners. This only highlighted his strong belief in the sovereignty of God— that God is in complete control of all things, including man's salvation. His task was to plant and water the gospel, but it was God who caused the growth.

A constant threat to John while travelling was getting sick. At any given moment, it seemed as though one town or another was battling an outbreak of disease or plague—and often resulted in the death of many within each community that it affected.

Sickness usually came in waves upon the people in Bedford. During some years, the town suffered more deaths from illness than others. In the spring of 1658, however, sickness found its way into the Bunyan's home once again. This time, though, it fell upon Mary.

Mary had just given birth to their fourth child and was now crippled by illness and John was dreading the worst.

As he sat watching Mary's chest slowly rise and fall, thoughts of how he could possibly make it with four children by himself passed through his mind.

Streams of sweat poured down the sides of Mary's face and John felt utterly helpless. A doctor came by, but offered no real cure and he immediately missed John Gifford. 'He would know what to do,' John thought to himself.

As the afternoon sun began to sink below the window seal, John's heart sank while watching his wife of ten years die in front of him.

John knelt by her bed and grabbed her hand with his. With his chin quivering, he looked at his wife. 'Mary, if you can hear me, I want you to know that I love you. Death can do no harm to you. It is only a passage out of a prison into a palace, out of a sea of troubles into a haven of rest. Go boldly into your rest, Mary. Pass through the river and I'll see you in the celestial city.'

Mary's death was heard to bear, but God blessed him with many friends and much support from his

Bedford church. The women of the church often cared for his children while he was away and many of the members would spend time with him while he was at home or even working in the shop. Mary, his eldest daughter of eight years old, though blind, could help with the other children as well.

He took the children down to see his father and step-mother in Elstow. His father still worked in his shop, fixing peoples' metal wares and making some of his own. They still lived in the same old house down the street from the Elstow church. After a short visit, they began walking back toward Bedford. As he passed by the church and the village green, he was reminded of his former life—a life he'd rather forget.

'How wretched I was,' he said to himself in disgust. 'How wretched I am still!' Memories of bell ringing and playing sports raced through his mind and Bunyan felt great remorse over his sin. He remembered playing soccer on Sunday and taunting others to join him. The trips down to Elstow were few due to John's preaching schedule and taking care of his children.

Oliver Cromwell's death in September 1658 sent the nation into a panic, many wondering if his incompetent son, Richard, would be able to defend her against a hostile European continent.

The crisis situation only enhanced Bunyan's preaching. The only true hope and security was in Christ Jesus. And people flocked to hear the preacher.

One day, while travelling on horseback from Cambridge where he had been preaching, a stocky gentleman wearing a dark gown stepped in front on his horse with his hands raised.

'Woa,' John blurted, pulling back hard on the reins. John looked down at the man and could tell— by his academic garb—that he was a professor from the university.

'Are you Mr Bunyan?' the man asked, looking up at John.

John turned his horse to the side so he could see the man better. He was furrowing his forehead. 'Yes, I am,' John replied.

'Might I have a word with you concerning your preaching?'

John thought the question was a little odd considering the circumstances, but nodded anyway. 'Of course,' honestly expecting a compliment or the like.

'How dare you preach the Scriptures without the original Greek and Hebrew languages!' the man quipped. John sat up straight on his horse and continued to listen. 'A true preacher would search the original languages of the Bible before even stepping into a pulpit. You, however, are doing a disservice to the church by starving the flock of God!'

John was both amazed and hurt by the professor's comment. 'May I ask you a question, sir?'

'Go on.'

'Do you, sir, have the original manuscripts written by the prophets and apostles?'

The man stepped back a little and grumbled a little under his breath. 'Well, no. Of course not, but I do believe I have true copies of the originals.'

'And I,' said Bunyan, 'believe the English Bible to be a true copy also, sufficiently translated from the originals. If neither you nor I have the original manuscripts, you cannot make such a charge of my preaching.'

'Ah,' the man replied pointing his finger into the air. 'But I have heard of the awful effects of your preaching even here in Cambridge. People say that you are not charitable toward your hearers—calling many unbelievers who have been baptized.'

John nodded and stabilized his horse, 'That is true, my friend.'

'On what grounds can you make such a claim?' The professor was obviously angry.

John smiled. 'Dear Sir, baptism doesn't guarantee salvation. We are saved by faith alone in the finished work of Christ. It is faith that I am insisting on, though I do call all who profess the true religion to be baptized.'

'You are uncharitable at best,' the man retorted. And with that, he gave a short angry breath through his nose and walked passed John toward Cambridge. To many, being a Dissenter and public teacher, without going through the usual course of education and ordination, was an unpardonable offence.

John had mixed emotions. Part of him did want to go to university to learn the Bible better and the ancient languages, but another part of him felt called already to gospel ministry.

John honoured the learned godly as Christians, but preferred the Bible before the libraries of all the universities. Even though he would sometimes desire more education, he saw much idolatry in human learning. It frequently confused and impeded the gospel.

John looked back to the vanishing professor. 'Words easy to be understood do often hit the mark,' he thought to himself. 'High and learned ones only pierce the air.'

And with that, he set his face toward Bedford.

It was autumn 1659 and the leaves spread their many colours, from golden yellow to bright red. Like so many other preachers and parishioners alike, Bunyan usually awoke early in the morning to pray and commune with God. He also poured himself into the Holy Scriptures—studying and applying its message to his life. The mornings of early autumn were cool enough to awaken a tired body.

'Lord, I am tired and need your strength this new day,' John prayed. He was sitting on the ground along the outside of a rock wall. The sunlight was making its way across the horizon to the east and John took in a deep refreshing breath.

He thought of all that was happening in his life—his preaching schedule, his writing and even some feelings of loneliness.

He looked up at the sky. 'Lord God, is it right that I should feel this longing for another helper and wife?' He tried to search his heart for any sin surrounding such a desire. He thought maybe part of it was selfishness, but it was nevertheless a true desire for a companion.

Feeling a sense of comfort, he kicked his feet out in front of him and began to think through women whom he could possibly pursue and eventually found himself thinking of a certain young lady named Elizabeth, naturally named after the great Protestant queen.

Elizabeth was one of the early members of the Bedford church, attending before John arrived on the scene. She was only a little over one year older than he, born around 1630.

During the 1650s, Elizabeth watched John care for his family and especially admired the way he tended to the needs of his blind daughter, Mary. When his wife died, she felt awful and secretly desired to help personally, although she knew that such a move would seem rather inappropriate.

As John sat against the wall, his thoughts of Elizabeth seemed to race and his desire to pursue her deepened. He knew she was single, healthy and committed to Christ her Lord. Though she was generally shy and quiet, she had a deep compassion for people that often took bold initiatives.

Before the year's end, John and Elizabeth courted and married. They set themselves to a life together and she was all too eager to care for his four children. But all too often, disaster punctures joy and the newly married couple found themselves in the clutch of Satan's evil schemes.

Arrested!

Elizabeth sat in an old wooden chair knitting near the fireplace. The children had already fallen asleep and she was beginning to wonder when John would return home.

It was not that uncommon for John to be out late. Even after working all day with metal or preaching at a nearby town, he would often walk several miles just to talk with a family about the treasures of the gospel.

Elizabeth had to completely trust in God's provision for her new husband, though she feared for his life. Walking around at night was a dangerous mission—especially during the turbulent winter of 1660. After the deposition of Richard Cromwell, the nation was on the brink of all-out anarchy. The Lords and ministers knew they needed to act quickly to stabilize the country and the only answer that came was to call back the monarchy.

Charles II had escaped to France in 1651 after being defeated by Parliamentary armies at Worcester. To many Royalists, he had been their king since the beheading of his father Charles I in 1649. But with the death of Oliver Cromwell, the inability of Richard

Cromwell and the inevitable collapse of society, the nation pleaded for Charles II to return as their king. So in May 1660, Charles was proclaimed King of England, Scotland and Ireland.

Suddenly, the pendulum that had swung in favour of the puritans and the English Reformation now swung back toward an Episcopal church government, which supported the king as supreme governor of the church, the *Book of Common Prayer* as the official liturgy and, significantly, the removal of all those preachers who 'got in the way'—namely, the Puritans. These anti-Puritan laws became known as the Clarendon Code, designed to shore up the position of the established Church of England as the true church in the British Isles.

Within a few months, trials were held for the thirty-one of fifty-nine Commissioners who had signed the death warrant of Charles I in 1648. Twelve were condemned to death by being hung drawn and quartered. It was a brutal execution process that struck fear in all who opposed the new king. Even Cromwell's body was dug up and suspended by chains at Tyburn.

The old Episcopal clergy, who had been ousted with the rise of Cromwell, now came forward in throngs—insisting that they be reinstated to the livings from which they had been banished.

It was no longer safe for preachers to preach openly without a license issued by the official state church. Ministers had to sign a statement declaring that they held to the thirty-nine Articles of Faith as prescribed in the *Book of Common Prayer*. They had to agree to bring back the vestments, altars and the worshipping of the bread and wine.

John Bunyan and the pastor of the Bedford church, John Burton, had to let the authorities take over St John's church building. Suddenly, the members—including the Bunyans—had nowhere to meet and the deacons scrambled to figure out what to do. Families opened up their homes for several weeks, but many declined due to fear of being fined...or worse.

But when they thought that the situation couldn't get any worse, Burton died in September 1660. Now, all eyes turned to young Bunyan to lead them in those turbulent times.

Despite the dangers, John continued to preach and teach the gospel. His popularity as a preacher and as an author still brought him many secret invitations to preach and exhort fellow believers in the Lord. However, such popularity also marked him as a target for harassment and questioning.

He would go to barns and houses to preach. When the authorities approached the meeting houses, friends would help him escape into the night. Sometimes, he dressed up in various costumes so as to disguise himself and travel on horseback to meet a secret group of anxious listeners.

The night that Elizabeth sat knitting by the fire, then, was not uncommon. But that fact certainly did not set her fears aside. This particular night late in November 1660, he had been invited to preach to a group in Samsell in Bedfordshire, which was about thirteen miles south of Bedford.

After a while of knitting and waiting, she retired to bed.

Later that night, while Elizabeth was fast asleep, she was startled by three loud knocks on her door. She sprung up and reached over to the other side of the bed where John slept, but he wasn't there!

'Where is he?' she thought to herself.

She jumped up out of bed and tried to catch her breath. She could hear her heart beating in her ears and, with trembling hands, lit a small lamp that hung out from the wall. As she walked toward the front door, another set of three loud knocks pounded against the door and this time the children slowly emerged from their room.

'Get back to bed!' she said with a forceful whisper, pointing to their room.

Elizabeth unlatched and slowly opened the door to find a tall man with a dark moustache and frightful eyes who held a lantern up next to his face. She didn't recognize him.

'Elizabeth?' the man asked.

'Yes…I am she.' She knew something was terribly wrong.

'I am sorry.' He paused. 'It is John. He has been arrested!'

* * *

The small group of Christian friends sat around the Bunyan's living room trying to describe what had happened, but Elizabeth's loud weeping kept interrupting their story.

'Mrs Bunyan,' one of the older men started. 'Last night's service was at a farmhouse in Samsell. It was in the middle of a field surrounded by elm trees and we thought it would be the safest place for—'

'Safe?' Elizabeth retorted, with glaring anger and confusion. 'Was there a warrant for his arrest that you did not know about?'

The man cleared his throat. 'Yes...yes, we did know about a warrant, Elizabeth.' He looked at the others who all looked down at the floor and then back at Elizabeth. 'But John didn't.'

'Why didn't you tell him?' Elizabeth demanded.

'But we did, soon after he arrived. He knew then that Francis Wingate the local magistrate wanted to arrest him for preaching. But he stood up and told everyone present to come and be of good cheer— that our cause is good and we need not be ashamed of it. He told everyone that to preach God's Word is so good a work that we shall be rewarded even if we suffer for it. He had time to run, but he chose not to. He felt that if he ran, it would only hinder the gospel and send the wrong message to the people assembled. I think he wanted to assure us that the gospel is worth living for...and dying for.'

Elizabeth was confused, angry and incredibly proud—all at the same time. Wiping her face with a small cloth, she glanced around at the men again. 'When did the authorities come?'

'John opened the meeting with prayer, prayer like we have never heard before—real, deep and fully dependant upon God. We opened our Bibles with him and he began to preach from the ninth chapter of the Gospel of John.'

'Go on,' Elizabeth said with earnestness.

'As he proceeded to speak to the people, the constable, with Mr Wingate's men, came in upon us, ordering John to stop and go with them. He did so, but exhorted us as he was leaving to take courage and to trust in the Lord Jesus Christ.'

'Where is he now?'

'He is in the hall apartment of Mr Wingate's house, being questioned as we speak.'

Elizabeth looked down at the floor and anxiously tugged at the cloth in her hands. Her hopes of a peaceful life with John were now dashed against the rocks of persecution and state authority. She began to think about how she was to support herself and the children if something happened to John, but those thoughts began to vanish when she considered her hope in the Lord's provision.

'God will take care of us. He is enough and he is our Treasure,' she thought to herself.

* * *

Mr Wingate peered at John whose hands were tied behind him. The constable stood nearby holding a long rifle in front of him.

'What were you doing at this farmhouse in Samsell?' Wingate asked, squinting his eyes.

'I was simply instructing the people, pleading with them to flee their sins and run to Christ.'

At this, Wingate lost his temper. 'I will break the neck of such meetings!'

'It might be so,' John replied, 'but you cannot stop the Gospel from going forth.'

Wingate looked over to the constable. 'I hereby issue a bond for this rebel and if he shall preach again, he shall be put in the County Gaol*.'

'You might as well send me there now.' John's voice was unwavering. 'I cannot and will not refrain from preaching the Word of God!'

At this, Wingate stormed out of the room to draw up papers for Bunyan's placement in the Bedford gaol. Just then, Wingate's brother-in-law, William Foster, entered and tried to persuade Bunyan to leave the task of preaching. He gave John the usual argument that only those with the support of the bishop and parliament should preach Christ's gospel.

Bunyan had the support of neither. But it didn't trouble him. He had been called by God to preach! There was little further argument.

* An early English term for *jail*.

When Wingate returned with papers in his hand, he looked at John and the constable. 'Follow me.'

The three of them walked out of the hall and climbed into a wooden horse-pulled carriage. Nobody said much on the way to Bedford. All three looked out of the window at the early morning landscape. The air was unusually dry and cold and John's mind and heart were racing. As the sunlight stretched across the fields, he took a deep breath and tried to prepare himself for whatever might await him at the gaolhouse. He thought of his family too.

'Lord, protect Elizabeth and my children. Give me strength for what lies ahead.'

They passed through Elstow and John saw his father's house. He was tempted to yell something, but such an attempt seemed futile. He also saw the Elstow church and thought about the irony of his present situation. It was strange how now that he was saved and preached God's Word he was in trouble with the authorities. It had nothing to do with Sunday sports and his night-time bell-ringing!

'Perhaps I do not get along with authority,' John thought to himself with a slight smile.

They crossed the Bedford Bridge and stopped in front of an old rock chapel at the corner of High Street and Silver Street in Bedford. But it was no longer a chapel as it had been converted into a gaol.

As Mr Wingate explained the situation to the soldiers standing outside, the constable led John through the front door and into a large one-room cell. A massive door made of three transverse layers of oak and fastened through with iron bolts had bars across an open centre. As John walked into the cell, about thirty other prisoners greeted him—all sitting around either on the floor or on wooden benches. He looked over and saw another thirty prisoners in an adjacent cell.

The County Gaol consisted mainly of a ground floor and first floor. The ground floor was occupied by felons and had two day rooms, besides sleeping rooms. There were also two dungeons underground. One, in total darkness, was reached by a descent of eleven steps. The first floor, which was for debtors, consisted of four sleeping rooms and one common day room. All the rooms were 8 ½ feet (2.5908 metres) high. Outside the Gaol was a small courtyard where any of the prisoners could go and mingle.

John looked around the crowded room and noticed a row of iron-gated windows facing Silver Street. He took a deep breath and almost gagged; the smell of body odour, urine and stale air filled the room.

'Clank.' The constable fastened the door behind him.

John walked over to the wall with the windows and looked out on the street. The town was already bustling with business. Although he knew he had done the right thing, Satan began to tempt him with thoughts of guilt and shame. He longed to see his wife and children.

By mid-morning, the news that Bunyan was in gaol spread through the town. John sat down on the damp floor—due to a leak in the ceiling—and scanned the room. A nail was wedged in the corner closest to where he was sitting. Without standing up, he stretched over and picked it up, feeling the sharp point with his finger.

Turning around toward the wall, he began to scratch his thoughts and feelings right there on the wall:

'Here I lie waiting the good will of God to do with me as he pleases, knowing that not one hair of my head can fall to the ground without the will of my Father who is in heaven; that, let the rage and malice of men be what they may, they can do no more and go no farther than God permits them; and even when they have done their worst, we know that all things work together for good for them that love God.'

A trial date was set for the second week of January 1661, eight weeks after his arrest. It was to be held in an old building known as the Chapel of Herne, which was located near the grammar school.

The people of Bedford and even from the surrounding communities and towns were anxious due to the fact that this was the first trial for a Nonconformist preacher since Charles II returned to England as king.

* * *

The county magistrates who sat on the bench at John's trial were predisposed against him. Some of them had been put in gaol by Puritan leaders and others had been persecuted under the reign of Cromwell. One of them, Sir John Kelynge, had even taken part in the trial condemning the regicides who executed Charles I. Of all the people who could sentence someone like Bunyan to gaol, these magistrates were possibly the most biased.

The trial was swift and concluded with the following charge:

'You, John Bunyan, are indicted for devilishly and perniciously abstaining from coming to church to hear divine service, and for being a common upholder of several unlawful meetings and conventicles to the great disturbance and distraction of the good subjects of this kingdom, contrary to the laws of our sovereign lord the King.'

After hearing the charge, Bunyan cracked a smile. 'That is quite amazing that the little meeting at Samsell is described in such ponderous and awful terms,' he thought to himself.

The clerk of the court peered at John. 'What have you say to this charge, Mr Bunyan?'

'Sir, indeed I did go to the church that you have said and, by God's grace, was a member with the people over whom Christ is the head.'

'But do you come to church, you know what I mean; to the parish church to hear divine service?'

119

Kelynge impatiently asked. The Bedford church that John had been called to as a deacon was not an 'established' church by the government. It had no priest or bishop and certainly did not use the *Book of Common Prayer* during the services.

'No sir,' John replied.

The debate that followed between John and the magistrates came to a head when they finally asked him directly about using the Prayer Book.

'The *Book of Common Prayer* is filled with good things,' John said. 'But for my part, I pray very well without it.'

'Sedition!' one man on the bench blurted. 'If he is against the Prayer Book, then he is against the established Church in England. And if Bunyan is against the established Church in England, then he is against the King of England!'

Kelynge looked at John. 'You are possessed with the spirit of delusion and of the devil! You shall never preach again! Where is your license for preaching and on what authority do you go about preaching?'

'On the authority of Jesus Christ! The first epistle of Peter, chapter four, states that each has received a gift from God. My gift is preaching the Word.'

'Your gift is not determined by you!' Kelynge snapped back. 'Do you or do you not confess to the charge against you this day?'

Bunyan cleared his throat, standing before this bench of angry men. 'My friends and I have held many meetings together. We have enjoyed the sweet comforting presence of the Lord among us and I have led as a deacon, a servant of Jesus Christ, in His church here in Bedford for many years, as some of you well know. But here I stand guilty before you, yet not guilty before God.'

'Hear your judgment then,' Kelynge gruffed. 'You must be taken back to prison and there lie for three months following, and if then you do not submit to go to church and leave off preaching, you must be banished from this realm.'

John took a deep breath and thought of life without Elizabeth.

'If, after such banishment you are again found in the country without special license from the King, you shall be stretched by the neck and hang.' Then pointing to John, Kelynge ordered the gaoler to remove the prisoner from among them.

After three months in prison, a certain official named Mr Cobb, came to John and pleaded with him to recant.

'Please, Mr Bunyan, for the sake of your family and for the peace and purity of this town, submit yourself to the church and to the crown.'

'I am willing to submit to the church and to the crown in so far as the Lord Christ remains the Head. But Christ has called me to preach his gospel and I cannot and will not resist His call.' John was more determined than ever to defend the meetings he had preached at and to defend his right to preach the Word of God.

Mr Cobb's efforts were futile—Bunyan remained resolute. Instead of being banished from the realm, Bunyan simply remained in the County Gaol due to the excitement and business surrounding the coronation of King Charles. It was as if Bunyan was simply overlooked.

During the summer of 1661, Elizabeth appealed three times to have her husband released. On one occasion, she was able to make it into an actual court hearing on the matter. She pleaded to the magistrates that he did not disturb the peace and that she had four children—one of them blind—to look after.

'How are you able to live?' a judge asked her.

Tears were flowing down her face. 'My children and I are only alive now because of generous people from our fragmented church. Please release my husband. Please let him come home to me.'

'Will he promise to refrain from preaching?'

Elizabeth paused and then spoke with an unwavering voice. 'As long as my husband has a voice, he will preach the gospel of Christ to the glory of our God and Father.'

Upon hearing this, the magistrates condemned the prisoner to remain in gaol and Elizabeth left for her lonely cottage alone and frightened.

Shivering with Shoelaces

'Kaboom!' Thunder ripped through the room where John slept. The lightning lit up the night sky, sending flashes of light through the one window of his room, which he shared with eleven other prisoners.

John pulled up his thin quilt over his face and felt the tip of his nose with his finger. 'I am so cold,' he thought to himself. A sudden chill shot down the length of his spine and John curled up trying to keep his body heat contained. The gaol had no fire place—it was too much 'trouble' for the gaoler to collect wood.

Because he was new to prison life, he didn't get fresh straw for his sleeping mat. Those that had been there the longest had 'seniority.' The gaoler was given a mere £5 a year to purchase straw for the prisoners, which meant that after six months of a mat's constant use, a prisoner might as well be sleeping on the floor. This particular night, in the late winter of 1662, was incredibly lonely. Even though he had made a few friends in the short time he was in gaol, he missed Elizabeth and his children more than ever, especially his blind daughter. They visited occasionally, but it certainly wasn't the same as being at home and sleeping under the same roof.

'Kaboom!' Another crack of thunder shook the building.

John pulled the quilt back down just below his eyes so he could see out the little window. 'Lord, be with my wife and children tonight. Please protect them and let them know that you love them.'

The amazing thing about John's imprisonment was that, at any moment, he could have been released—if he promised not to preach. The conditions of prison life seemed to be like one wave after another pounding his shore of faith and hope. And there were nights when he felt that he couldn't take it any more. It was too cold, too miserable. But, in the midst of his pain and temptation to renounce his holy calling, he felt the Lord Jesus telling him, 'My grace is sufficient for thee, for my power is made perfect in thy weakness.' John took a deep breath, exhaled and watched his breath form a cloud of vapour above him. 'I wonder if I will be out of here soon,' he thought to himself. He closed his eyes and fell asleep.

John certainly had to do something. His family was struggling to make ends meet from the handouts of friends. He looked around the cell filled with prisoners who were talking, reading or just staring into the air.

It was mid-April 1662 and the afternoon warmth was welcomed by all. He noticed one older prisoner weaving a set a small strings together and sat down beside him on the oak floor.

'What are you making, my friend?' John asked, trying to figure it out before he answered.

'Laces, long-tagged shoelaces.' The man didn't stop at John's question. 'I have some friends who sell them for me and so I make them to support my family.'

John had heard of shoes with laces, but had never seen any before. Most shoes had a buckle on them, but he had heard that more people were using laces to tie their shoes as of late.

'I purchase the twine from Ely's Shop off the square and friends pick up the metal bits used at the end of the laces.'

John immediately thought of his own family and how they were struggling. 'May I try it?'

'Indeed,' the man said handing the strands over to John.

John placed the tied end of the three small strands under his boot and wove them together. 'Like this?' he asked.

'That's right.' The man paused. 'Make sure the weave is tight.'

After about two feet in length, the man handed John two long thin sheets of metal. 'Now wrap each end with one of these and press the metal together with your boot.' He waited for John to do so. 'There you have it,' the man said picking up the other end. 'A long-tagged shoelace!'

John was excited. 'Do you think I could make some and sell them too?'

'Indeed.' The old man smiled and looked at John. 'They are used for other things besides shoes, you know. Everybody needs strong pieces of thin rope.'

Within a week, John had collected some twine and metal sheets by asking visitors and friends for the material. And there began John's new trade as a maker of long-tagged shoelaces. The tinker in Elstow had turned shoelace maker in prison. Though it didn't amount to much, it did help support his family.

During the late summer of 1662, tensions came to a head in Parliament against Nonconformist ministers in England. As far as Parliament was concerned, the stability of the kingdom was threatened by these 'ministers' of the gospel who did not submit to the official state church nor did they see the benefit of using the *Book of Common Prayer*—the official liturgy in the worship of the established church.

On 24 August, St Bartholomew's Day, nearly 1,700 ministers were ejected from the Church of England—most of them Puritans. Many of them were fined and their possessions taken. Some were even thrown immediately into prison. In Bedford, the already crowded Gaol swelled to over-capacity.

Some who joined Bunyan in gaol were well-known ministers like John Donne, William Wheeler and John Wright. Donne, for his part, preached at night for fear of being arrested. On one of these occasions, officers of the law surprised the meeting and they marched the whole body of them, nearly sixty in number, off to Bedford Gaol.

The irony is that this only created more instability across the nation due to the fact that each of these ministers had considerable influence and popularity among the general population. It seemed, once again, that the nation was on the brink of anarchy.

If it were not for the peaceful leaving of these ministers from their positions and parishes, there might have been some damaging opposition to the crown.

With the prison population increasing disease became a deadly reality. It was during times of great distress that the prisoners turned to Bunyan to hear God's Word taught and applied. In fact, during the day, the big rooms on the ground floor would also serve as chapels and John regularly preached the Word right there in the gaol.

The reason that he was in gaol in the first place was for preaching in public. Even though many saw this as 'preaching,' the authorities didn't see this as preaching in public, and for that reason, he was able to get away with it.

Materials for shoelaces weren't the only things John's wife and friends brought to him. They also brought paper, pens, ink and books. Depending on who was standing guard, John had considerable freedom—sometimes even to walk around town.

The gaolers were also fairly lenient on who visited him. Many in his church, who were now meeting secretly in a member's home, visited him and brought him writing materials and the latest books and pamphlets.

It must be understood that it wasn't just those in the Gaol who sought Bunyan's spiritual guidance and counsel, many came from outside the Gaol to seek the advice of the famous preacher. During the autumn of 1662, many who joined John in the Gaol were fellow preachers and ministers of the gospel who had been forced to leave their parishes. So most of the people in the Gaol were believers in Christ and still desired to be fed from God's Word. John was perfectly willing to rise to the occasion.

'Friends, we are cast down for praying honest prayers to God without the Prayer Book.' John's voice was sincere and urgent as he addressed his fellow prisoners.

'We are cast down for serving people in the name of Christ Jesus our Lord. We are put in chains for preaching from the Holy Scriptures. The world, the flesh, and the Devil have set their arrows against the saints of God, but we shall not lose hope.'

'Amen!' several of the men responded.

'We shall not lose hope,' John continued, 'for Christ endured the cross on our behalf. Hebrews 12 tells us that we are to 'look to Jesus, the Founder and

Perfecter of our faith, who for the joy that was set before Him endured the cross.'

As John preached, he noticed that even one of the gaolers had stepped in to listen.

'As we have been placed in chains unjustly, so Christ endured the greatest injustice the world has ever known—his crucifixion. Run to Christ, even now. Run to Him as the Perfecter of your faith!'

After John had finished, a few of the men were crying and others were praying. The sight was only a testimony to the Spirit of God working in a mighty way.

John usually wrote his sermons down on loose-leaf sheets of paper. Many of these hand-written prison sermons eventually found their way into the form of 'prison books'—one of the earliest being *Praying in the Spirit*. The book was a treatise on prayer.

'Prayer', John wrote, 'is the opener of the heart to God and a means by which the soul, though empty, is filled.' The book, which was published in 1663, was a sort of prison manifesto against using the forms of prayer found in the *Book of Common Prayer*. During the early 1660s, John and other Nonconformist ministers found it rather easy to publish a work, especially if they were well known among the people.

John argued in *Praying in the Spirit* that we are not to pray according to a man-made book full of form and structure, but according to the Holy Spirit, who was at work within us. Bunyan felt that the prayers in the established church, following the Prayer Book, were empty and said in vain because the hearts of the people were not in it.

One summer night in 1665, John sat down on his straw mat to begin writing his own autobiography, *Grace Abounding to the Chief of Sinners*. With the candle flickering next to him, he began to recount the events of his life—from his rebellious days as a teenager to the days of his arrest and imprisonment.

So began his journey into his own past. He documented the way God had faithfully brought him out of his bondage to sin into, ironically, a state of true freedom. He was free, though he was in prison—because his true freedom was found in the finished work of his Saviour Jesus Christ.

But the publishing of his autobiography in 1666 was greeted with some of the worst days in the history of England. It was as if Satan had roused himself from hell to torment the people and nobody seemed prepared for what was about to happen.

'What is your business coming to Bedford so late at night?' the constable asked the rider who had a panicked look on his face.

'It's the plague,' the man said breathing heavily. 'It has made its way into Elstow and it will be in Bedford before long. We need to evacuate the town immediately!'

The rider passed over the bridge and made his way to the alehouses. Suddenly, people emerged from all over looking up and down the street—asking each other whether or not they should leave. Unfortunately, the poor didn't have a choice. They couldn't leave. Not only did they not have a fast mode of transportation, they lived 'hand to mouth' and had nothing stored up for an extended time away from home.

When John heard some yelling, he stood up—with some of the other men in his cell—and looked through his iron-barred window toward the courtyard. To the north side, he could see part of Silver Street, which was bustling with people carrying lanterns.

'I wonder what is happening,' one of the men said.

John paused. 'I don't know, but it does not look good, my friend.'

Suddenly, the gaoler appeared in front of their sleeping cell. 'Gentlemen. I have some very hard news to tell you. The plague that has been ravishing London has made its way to Elstow and is expected to break out here any day…and it might already be here.'

John felt his stomach turn over. He knew what that meant. The first to die were usually those living in insanitary quarters with a lot of people—like him!

The gaoler grabbed the thick bars holding the prisoners in their cell and pressed his face to the door. 'I'm sorry, but you have to stay here. There's nothing I can do.' Even though everyone in the room knew that already, it still came as a surprise.

After the gaoler walked away, John turned to the other men. 'Let us pray together.'

The plague that had begun from infected rats coming from Dutch trading ships carrying bales of cotton was now ravishing the country. In some cases, like the village of Eyam in Derbyshire, the plague took the lives of nearly 75% of the inhabitants.

By mid-1666, the plague had killed 75,000 to 100,000 people across England. As expected, many prisoners died. Although less than some towns, Bedford didn't miss its presence—taking almost fifty people plus some whose deaths were not recorded.

Despite the tragedy of the plague, it was not the only major event of 1666. The nation stood in shock and horror at what would amount to one of the most significant disasters in the history of England—the Great Fire of London.

At midnight, on 2 September 1666, a fire started at the bakery of Thomas Farriner on Pudding Lane in London. London, at this time, was overcrowded and many of the houses still had thatched roofs and wood exteriors. The wind—being particularly strong that night—blew the fire to the adjacent buildings and for the next three days continued to burn most of London.

By 5 September, the fire had consumed 13,200 houses, 87 churches, St Paul's Cathedral and most of the city's authority buildings. Nearly 90% of the inhabitants of London suddenly became homeless and, although nobody knows how many people died, it was the worst fire in London's history.

Fear spread through the country of foreign attack at a time when they were most vulnerable. The nation was at war with the Dutch and many believed they had ignited the fire before launching a massive attack. Others believed it was God's displeasure with the current king, Charles II. Still others were simply scared and didn't know what to think.

The death from the plague and the Great Fire of London sent many people asking questions about God and the nature of evil and suffering. If God is all powerful and good, how could he let such things happen?

John suddenly became a popular preacher and counsellor once again—in prison. He assured his fellow prisoners that God was still powerful and good. He assured them that the present sufferings of this world point us to the suffering Servant, Jesus Christ. These sufferings point us to a day when there will be no more tears or pain and when the present realities will give way to a new heaven and a new earth.

Without warning, John was released from prison during the Autumn of 1666. In the midst of the upheaval surrounding the disasters of the Plague and Fire, a brief pardon was granted toward Nonconformist ministers in Bedford's Gaol. So many people needed guidance that the 'official' ministers of the gospel couldn't respond to the needs and attention of the people.

But before a month had passed, Bunyan was thrown back in prison. In the eyes of the authorities, he was dangerous. He had too many followers and did not submit to the liturgy of the Church of England. What were they to do but to throw him back into prison?

How was John able to carry on? How was he able to stand the awful conditions of prison life knowing that with one simple statement he would be set free? What drove him to act with such boldness and confidence? To all of these questions, it was nothing other than the power of Christ within him. In his weakness, John found strength. In the prison, he found freedom. In the darkness, he found light. And in his prayers, he found hope—hope that carried him on.

The Preacher Released

John could hear a heavy set of footsteps coming down the wood hallway toward his cell. In an instant, three men stopped in front of the iron-barred room and the tallest spoke.

'John Bunyan,' he called with a firm voice.

John stood up from an oak bench resting against the wall. 'Yes, sir.'

The man motioned to the gaoler and the gaoler unlocked the cell door. 'Please come with us.'

John was suddenly terrified. Though the political tides were changing in his favour, he knew that at any moment he could be hanged for 'treason,' if the authorities wanted to. He had prepared himself for being hanged many times and this time was no different—except that he had never been individually called out like this before.

John followed the three men down the hallway and outside the Gaol. When he walked out, the sun almost blinded him. He squinted his eyes and saw a number of people staring at him and another wave of fear hit him. 'Is this the end?' he thought to himself.

The man who had addressed him earlier stood directly in front of John and John looked to see if any armed men or military stood nearby.

'Mr Bunyan,' the man said, reading from a small piece of paper in his hands. 'March 1672, by order of Whitehall, you are hereby released from Bedford Gaol and pardoned for all crimes against the English crown.'

At this, the man looked up at John and cracked a smile. 'You are free to go, John.'

John's knees buckled and he fell to the ground weeping. He had been a prisoner for twelve years, since 1660, for preaching the gospel of Jesus Christ. Now, John was a free man.

Not only was Bunyan released from prison, but within two months, he was officially licensed to preach and teach by Parliament.

Two months later, in May, another message greeted Bedford.

The rolled-up sheet of paper sailed through the air and landed in the dirt at the doorstep of the Constable's building. The rider who had thrown it didn't stop, but immediately turned around and headed back out of Bedford.

Bending over, the gaoler outside picked up the roll, untied the small ribbon holding it together and stretched it out in front of him.

King Charles & c. To all Mayors, Bailiffs, Constables, and Others, and Military Whom it May Concern, Greeting.

The gaoler knew that this was straight from the top—from the king himself. He walked into the Constable's office and read the declaration:

In Pursuance of our Declaration of the 15th of March, 1672, We do hereby permit and license John Bunyan to be a Teacher of the Congregation allowed by Us in the House of Josias Roughed, Bedford, for the use of such as do not conform to the Church of England, who are of the persuasion commonly called Congregational. Given at our Court at Whitehall, the 9th day of May in the 24th year of our Reign, 1672,

By his Majesty's command,
Arlington

The royal Declaration of Indulgence of 1672 was Charles II's attempt to extend religious liberty to Nonconformists, like Bunyan. Many felt, however, that this was simply an indirect attempt to extend religious freedom to Roman Catholics living in England.

Charles secretly welcomed Catholicism and even his own brother, James (who would be the next king), openly declared himself a Catholic. While most people wanted to see their friends and family released from prison for being Nonconformist, they did not want to see Catholics in control. The last time a Catholic had ruled England was in the 1550s under Queen Mary, who earned herself the title 'Bloody Mary.'

Mary had ruled England with an iron fist— executing hundreds of Protestant believers. Stories had been passed down from one family to the next and England feared another Catholic monarch. In

1672, many feared foreign invasion from Catholic Spain or France.

But despite the nation's fears, Bunyan was freed and licensed to preach.

The mud slopped under John's feet as he ran toward his home. The late afternoon sun was turning orange and glowing on the roof tops of the houses on the west side of Bedford and a gentle breeze lifted John's hair with each pace.

As he ran, so many feelings began to flood his heart. For twelve years, he had been a prisoner. For twelve years, he had slept on a small straw mat on a cold hard floor. For twelve years, he had not enjoyed true freedom nor had he felt the unhindered embrace of his wife and family. Now, he was running home.

That night, around the dinner table, the Bunyan's enjoyed seared beef, fresh vegetables, warm bread and ripened fruit—compliments of members in his church. After dinner, they sang and prayed together, thanking God for sustaining them through suffering.

With full stomachs, the Bunyan family retired to bed. But John couldn't sleep. Not only was he thinking about all of the dark and lonely nights in the Gaol, he was thinking about his new task—ministering to the Bedford Church.

* * *

The church in Bedford, to which Bunyan had joined and ministered before his arrest, endured much hardship and persecution throughout the 1660s and early 1670s.

It was in 1660—when Charles II was crowned King of England—when their meeting place at St John's was taken from them and they were forced to meet in homes, barns and farm-houses.

Two years later, in 1662, Parliament passed the Act of Uniformity. This Act stated two requirements pertaining to Bunyan and other Nonconformist ministers like him. First, it required every minister in the Church to openly, publicly and solemnly read the morning and evening prayer, and after such reading, openly and publicly declare before the congregation his consent to everything contained in the *Book of Common Prayer*.

Secondly, the Act made ordination in the official state church mandatory for every minister in England. To be ordained, however, a minister had to subscribe to the King as the 'Supreme Governor' of the Church and subscribe to all the Articles of Faith in the *Book of Common Prayer*.

Nearly 1,700 ministers would not subscribe to these demands and were forced out of their livings and parishes.

Shortly after Charles was crowned king, John Burton, the minister of the Bedford Church, died. Suddenly, the church had no minister and no official place to meet. Though many wanted Bunyan to fill this spot, he was in gaol and could not adequately care for the people.

In 1663, the church called Samuel Fenne and John Whiteman to pastor the church, which began meeting in the home of John Fenne. Under their leadership, and by God's grace, the church began to grow.

On one side, people in England accepted the official state church form of government and conformed to its ritual and requirements. On the other side stood the Nonconformists, who, as they contended, on scriptural grounds, declined to do this and preferred a simpler and freer worship.

The policy of the Church towards Nonconformity was therefore to be a policy of stamping out. The little church in Bedford, despite many of its members being fined, continued and grew under persecution.

Even though Bunyan was in prison during these years while the church suffered, the members constantly sought his wisdom, advice and counselling. He was acting, though not officially, like their pastor. In 1670, the King passed the New Conventicles Act, which simply stated that any religious meeting of more than four people was illegal and its members subject to fines and imprisonment. Constables were given authority to break open doors to catch people meeting for worship. Such oppression, however, backfired and a new wave of resistance sparked against the King and the official state Church. The Nonconformists, for the most part, were peaceable people who just wanted to meet to worship God without being fined and many felt sorry for what was happening to them.

By the end of the summer 1671, seeing that public opinion was swinging in favour of the Nonconformists, the Bedford church began to consider the possibility of electing Bunyan to be their official pastor—even though he was still a prisoner.

Throughout his long imprisonment, John had grown mentally and spiritually—preaching, writing and counselling people in spiritual things. His influence stretched the whole of England through his many 'prison books' and when the members of the Bedford church needed a scribe to compose an important letter to authorities or for some other significant cause, they chose Bunyan for the job.

In October 1671, the Bedford church wrote down the following minutes from their meeting:

At a full Assembly of the Church at Bedford the 21ˢᵗ of the 10ᵗʰ month; after much seeking God by prayer, and sober conference formerly had the Congregation did at this meeting with joint consent call forth and appoint our brother John Bunyan to the pastoral office. And he accepting thereof, gave up himself to serve Christ and his Church in that charge; and received of the Elders the right hand of fellowship.

It was now nearly twelve years since the church of St John on the south side of the river was taken from them, and during all that time they had been homeless wanderers, meeting in each other's houses, and now in fields and woods.

After King Charles issued the Declaration of Indulgence—granting freedom to Nonconformists and after John was freed, the Church in Bedford quickly purchased a barn on an orchard off of Mill Lane to use as a place to meet and worship. The church was officially recognized by Whitehall and the King's seal gave it authority to meet and to worship for the first time in twelve years on 20 August 1672.

As Bunyan lay in bed thinking about his new position as pastor, he thought about the trials and hardships that he still might have to endure. But he knew that, as God had sustained him before, he would certainly sustain him again. So with joy and trust, John fell asleep in his own bed next to his own wife in his own house. For now, he was at rest.

'Where are your papers?' demanded Mr Overinge, the Mayor of Leicester. He was a short stocky man who seemed to care less about John's papers than about his own authority to ask the question.

John fished around his pocket and pulled out his preaching license. 'Here it is,' he smiled.

'John Bunyan. That is you, I suspect?'

'Yes sir.'

The man handed the paper back to John. 'Are you going to cause trouble here in Leicester?' He seemed to know something about John in the way he asked the question.

'No sir. I am here to preach in the house opposite St Nicholas' Church. They have invited me to share from God's Word this Lord's Day.'

The man grumbled, 'very well,' and walked across the road to a large brick home with a table out in front. The sign over the table read, 'Church-Ale.'

At that moment, John wished he had invited Mr Overinge to join them for the meeting.

As John stood up to address the small crowd assembled, he noticed that they were very attentive and eager to hear from God's Word. The sense of enthusiasm and joy gave him great confidence as he asked them to turn to the book of Romans, chapter 4.

Families all looked together at 'family Bibles' and the sound of shuffling paper came to a still.

'The Apostle Paul writes that Abraham believed God and it was credited to him as righteousness,' John began, gripping the sides of a make-shift wood pulpit. 'In the third chapter of Romans, we read that justification comes by faith alone. Here, God is telling us that the ground for our justification—for our being declared not guilty before a holy God—is that we are counted righteous. But how are we counted righteous?'

The people all looked at John, anticipating the answer.

'How are you counted righteous, I ask,' he said again, pausing. 'By faith in the One who is righteous on your behalf—Jesus Christ. The great Martin Luther once stated that justification by faith alone is the article on which the church stands or falls.'

John smiled and looked over the room of faces. 'Friends, today is no different. There are many who say that we earn righteousness by doing good works. But I say no! There has been only One who has earned the merits of righteousness and that person is our Lord Jesus Christ.'

At this, the room burst into a choir of 'Amens' and 'Hear, hears.'

'When Luther was asked to recant his writings concerning justification by faith alone, he told them that he was held captive by the Word of God and that to go against conscience is neither safe nor right. Here I stand; I can do no other. So help me God.'

At this, John looked up. 'Friends, today we are asked to take that stand again. We are asked to stand upon the Word of God as the only source of truth and revelation in our world. We are asked to stand against those who insist upon combining faith with works and combining the Word of God with the *Book of Common Prayer*. We are asked to take a stand for Christ in a fallen world.'

After he finished preaching many asked him to write his sermon down. To their wishes, by the winter of 1672, Bunyan had written a book entitled *A Defense of the Doctrine of Justification by Faith*.

Bunyan was a Puritan. He desired a thorough reformation of the Church in England to the extent that all the last remnants of Catholicism—the rituals, the corruption of the priests and bishops, the selling of indulgences and the authority of the pope—be cleared from the worship.

But John also strove for personal holiness and a passion to please God in his life. This is why he was so convicted over ringing the church bells or playing sports on the Christian Sabbath. These beliefs only grew stronger as he got older. He began to publish book after book about a variety of subjects, usually arising from the need to defend a doctrine of the faith or a certain viewpoint that someone had attacked him on.

The summer of 1673 was no different. The sacraments, namely the Lord's Supper and Communion, had taken centre stage in theological debate across the European Continent. Even among the Reformers—like Luther, Calvin and Zwingli— there was no unifying consensus.

From the beginning, the church in Bedford had taken a neutral position on baptism—they simply didn't hold baptism in high regard. They would certainly baptize people—children and adults—but they saw baptism as more of a sign of division than unity.

Many thought Bunyan to be a Baptist who would only baptize upon confession of Jesus Christ and was against infant baptism. But Bunyan himself had at least three of his own children baptized.

145

Bunyan wrote a response to numerous attacks on him in regard to baptism: 'I will not let water baptism be the rule, the door, the bolt, the bar, the wall of division between the righteous and the righteous.'

For those calling him a 'Baptist,' he replied, 'And since you would know by what name I would be distinguished from others, I would tell you I would be, and hope I am, a CHRISTIAN…'

As 1676 drew to a close, John's days became filled with the tasks of ministering to his people—caring for the sick, preaching, teaching, writing and counselling.

In November, he received word that his father was dying. John rode to Elstow where his father was stretched out in the upstairs bedroom. A doctor had come and gone and it was determined that Mr Thomas Bunyan was too ill to recover. It wasn't long before the man from whom John had learned his trade as a tinker and whom John had held in great respect died.

The loss, though difficult, only made him treasure Christ even more. Suffering had a way of taking all things on earth away—health, money and even life itself—so that a man may treasure Christ as one desired above all else.

As he rode home that night, the last part of Psalm 73 came to his head: '*Whom have I in heaven but thee, and there is none upon earth that I desire beside thee. My flesh and my heart (and my father's life) faileth, but God is the strength of my heart, and my portion forever.*'

The Perilous Progress of a Pilgrim

'Why?' Elizabeth screamed as four men cuffed John on the front steps of their cottage. The bitter January cold wasn't about to cool her hot temper.

'Your husband is charged with preaching without a proper license,' one of the men replied.

'A proper license?' Elizabeth piped with an angry tone. 'The only proper license should be issued by the Spirit of—'

'Elizabeth,' John said trying to ease her frustration. 'Justice will be served.'

'You best watch your words, Mrs Bunyan,' the man added with a deep voice.

At this, little Mary stepped out from inside the house. 'What is happening to father?'

Both John and Elizabeth paused and looked at their blind daughter and John's heart sank. 'It will be alright, Mary. I shall be back soon.'

The snow crunched in a rhythmic beat as the men led John toward the Bedford Gaol. As they marched along, nobody said anything. John knew there was nothing he could say—he knew that he lived and breathed solely by the mercy of God and that was his only source of comfort and hope. John saw the dark silhouette of the Gaol from some way off. He couldn't see any candle or lantern lit through outside windows—it looked particularly dark and cold. More than the fear of possible torture or death, John didn't want to spend another twelve years away from his family. The thought itself sent a chill down his spine.

King Charles' Declaration of Indulgence didn't last more than two years. By the end of 1673, it had been withdrawn and Nonconformists once again found themselves serving Christ under national persecution.

A warrant had been issued for Bunyan in March 1674, but was not put into effect until nearly three years later in early 1677. As soon as the Constable had received both word and permission to arrest John, he acted quickly and put him back into the Bedford Gaol.

The Indulgence withdrawn, all licenses previously granted to Nonconformists were recalled and deemed invalid. Only by conforming to the liturgy and practice of the Church of England could a person receive a 'proper' license. Moreover, all religious meetings that were not approved by the official Church were once again illegal.

One night, as the candle flickered beside him on his usual straw mat spread across the wood floor, he pulled out a few sheets of thick paper and a pen. He reflected on how God had brought him from a life of self-destruction and certain misery to a life that— though filled with struggle, pain and imprisonment— was joyful and full of meaning.

Despite his present condition in a cold prison cell in Bedford, he found comfort and hope in the future glory he would enjoy with Christ in heaven—the celestial city.

Glancing down at his paper, he began to write.

As I walked through the wilderness of this world, I lighted on a certain place, where was a Denn; And I laid me down in that place to sleep: And as I slept I dreamed a Dream. I dreamed, and behold I saw a Man clothed with Raggs, standing in a certain place, with his face from his own House, a Book in his hand, and a great burden upon his back...

And write he did, for six months. He poured out his understanding of the Christian life in the form of an allegory. An allegory is an extended story that represents reality. This allegory centred on a man named Christian and his journey from the City of Destruction to the Celestial City.

As he sat in gaol, looking at the iron bars that held him in his new 'home,' he remembered that this world was not his home and that he was simply passing through to a better world—a world without pain or suffering. He was a pilgrim in a foreign land. His real home was in heaven—that eternal place prepared by God for his people. John was just passing through until he reached the other side of the River, which symbolized death.

The story John wrote in that prison cell in Bedford told of the perilous progress of Christian—a pilgrim. It is told as a dream in which Christian, with a book in his hand and a heavy burden on his back, finds himself living in the City of Destruction. He also learns that he is condemned to death and judgment just by the very fact of his residence in the City of Destruction.

Being advised by a certain person named Evangelist, Christian flees toward a Wicket Gate and sets out on a journey, leaving behind his wife and children who refuse to accompany him. The course of his subsequent pilgrimage is full of danger and adventure. It takes him through treacherous sloughs, up steep mountains, across shadowy valleys and into dark castles, where he finds himself doubting the Christian faith.

He meets a friend along the way, named Faithful, who is eventually put to death at Vanity Fair for his faith in Christ Jesus. Despite this tragedy, Christian meets another friend, Hopeful, who accompanies him to the end. They face dragons, imprisonment and temptation. At length their pilgrimage ends when they pass through the River and enter the Celestial City. In Part Two of the allegory, Christian's wife, Christiana, and their children follow—overcoming many of the same obstacles that Christian faced.

The pilgrim's progress is from this world to that which is to come. As John wrote, he added many Bible references in the margins showing how the reality of Scripture matched Christian's life-journey in various places.

As Christian travelled in the story, so Bunyan told the story of conversion—following the theological steps of calling, justification, sanctification, perseverance and glorification. At the beginning, he is summoned by the Holy Spirit—though unbeknown to him—to leave the City of Destruction (calling). After leaving the City of Destruction, his heavy burden of sin falls off and he is set free (justification). His progress through the story shows his continual growth in becoming more like Christ Jesus (sanctification). Keeping his eyes fixed on Christ until the end (perseverance), Christian passes through the River and enters the Celestial City (glorification).

John brought to life the glorious truths of Scripture by telling a story. As he brought Christian and Hopeful through the River and into the Celestial City, something happened; something John didn't expect.

Looking out through the iron-barred window in his cell across Silver Street, John could see young boys running around. Apparently they had just been let out of the school house.

It was hot and muggy. The flies were abnormally bad—mainly due to the sour stench hovering in his cell. The June sun poured in through the window and John felt just plain miserable.

A group of men—four that he could count—were walking toward the Gaol. From the dark clothes he could tell that they were officials, though Bunyan couldn't quite tell exactly what sort.

A few moments later, he heard them saying something to the guard and in they came toward his cell, stopping directly in front of the door and looking through the bars. The other prisoners who shared the cell with Bunyan all stood up.

'Mr John Bunyan,' one of the men said in a strangely familiar tone.

John stepped forward and removed a wool cap. 'I am he.'

'Please come with us.'

'Did this just happen?' John thought to himself as he stepped out of the cell and followed the men down the hallway and out of the front door. The thought of being released quickly vanished when he realized that this could just as easily be his death sentence.

'It seems as though you have friends with power,' one of the men said, wiping his brow with his sleeve. 'Bishop Barlow has ordered your release thanks to Dr John Owen of Oxford.'

John couldn't believe what he was hearing.

'The law states that Bishop Barlow has the right to release a prisoner for nonconformity on a bond given by two persons that the prisoner would conform within six months. Assuming that you will conform, you are hereby released.'

John didn't know anything about this law and he had only briefly heard of Bishop Barlow. Barlow had just recently become Bishop over Bedfordshire after the death of the former Bishop Fuller.

The man speaking could tell that John was confused. 'The prisoner that Bishop Barlow has chosen, apparently at the request of Dr. Owen, is you, Mr Bunyan. You are free to get your things and go home. I have already spoken to the Constable and I will clear all this with the guard. Good day.'

'Thank you, sir.' John stuttered. He looked up at the afternoon sky and closed his eyes. 'Thank you, Lord, for Thy mercy and grace,' he prayed quietly.

John walked back into his cell, bundled his books and papers, said farewell to his fellow cell-mates and went home a free man once again.

Within a few months of being released from gaol, John found a publisher near Temple Bar and gave him his allegorical manuscript about the adventures of Christian. He titled the work *The Pilgrim's Progress from This World to That Which is to Come*.

The book went to print and was distributed all over England. Almost overnight, *The Pilgrim's Progress* had immediate fame and quickly became loved by both Nonconformists and official churchmen alike. But, as always, fame brought both admiration and attack.

Never before had Bunyan received so many invitations to come and preach or simply to come and talk to a crowd about his books. Letters poured in from all over the Kingdom seeking his counsel and presence. He was even invited to become a pastor in London.

But he had laboured and suffered with the people of Bedford for over twenty-five years. He had grown to love Bedford as his town and the people as his people. He was committed to Bedford until he died.

John was even able to approve worship meetings for Nonconformists for over twenty 'churches' meeting in houses, barns and open fields. That he became somewhat of a spiritual father to so many earned him the nickname—ironically—'Bishop Bunyan.'

The allegory of Christian progressing from this life to that which is to come was the story of every believer, in both the struggle and victory. Every Christian faces temptation, hardship and suffering. But, likewise, every believer also experiences a certain amount of joy because of his or her relationship with Christ, the King of kings and Lord of lords.

John grabbed his large iron tongs and gripped the glowing-red pot. Placing the pot on the anvil, his hammer came crashing down on the outside edge—shooting a spray of sparks across the work bench.

He finished banging and held the pot up in front of him, still using the large iron tongs. 'There,' he said to himself with a slight smile.

'John?' suddenly came a voice from the outside door of the workshop.

John turned around. 'Hey Elizabeth.' He could tell she looked troubled. 'Is everything alright?'

'Must you leave again? You just came home yesterday from preaching and now you are heading out in the morning. I feel like I don't see you.'

John put down the pot and tongs and took off his leather gloves. 'This is my passion, Elizabeth, and there are people that don't know Jesus as their Saviour and Lord.' He paused, though still looking at her. 'I must tell them.'

'But are there not other men who preach, John?'

John felt that he was getting nowhere. 'I know. You could come with me. We'll take the carriage and we can bring the children along as well.'

Elizabeth's face lit up. 'Really?' she said with a sense of excitement. John hadn't realized that Elizabeth even wanted to go.

The next morning, John, Elizabeth and the children loaded up in their carriage and left for Cambridge, where John had been invited to come and preach. He didn't know where they would be staying, but he knew that was part of the adventure—and part of their test of faith. Besides, he was just a pilgrim anyway.

The Tables Turn

The trees exploded with bright colour—red, yellow, orange and brown. The morning sun, which pierced the clear sky, cast a glow through the colourful leaves and warmed the crowd who were all huddling together trying to keep warm.

John jumped up on a large flat rock and flipped open a Bible, which he held straight out in front of him.

'My friends,' he began, scanning the faces of those assembled. '"The grass withers and the flowers fade, but the Word of the Lord shall abide forever." By His grace, may this Word of life be preached to you this morning.'

As John began to preach, several men scurried up the sloping hill and positioned themselves as lookouts. Even though Bunyan had been freed, there were many who were suspicious of his preaching and feared that he was inspiring crowds against King Charles or against the established authorities. Wealthy landowners paid spies to report any knowledge or suspicious activity of Bunyan.

The place where he preached was a large grassy basin surrounded by thick forest. The forest was only three hundred yards from the front gate of Preston Castle, which stood three miles east of Bedford. Bunyan had been invited by some of the people from the nearby town of Hitchin and, instead of meeting in a more public place, decided to preach to nearly three hundred eager listeners in a natural amphitheatre.

'King David wrote Psalm 51 after he had coveted his neighbour's wife, committed adultery, stole this wife from her husband, lied about it and then killed him.' John's voice was strong and confident—there was a sense of urgency that held everyone's attention. 'In doing this deed,' he continued, 'he broke five of the Ten Commandments.'

Some people stood and others sat on the grass, their eyes fixed on the preacher of the hour.

'But notice that David writes this Psalm to the choirmaster. It was to be sung publicly! But the Psalm is a prayer to God that God would blot out his transgressions and cleanse him from sin.'

John closed his Bible and tucked it under his arm. 'On what basis can the Lord cleanse a filthy sinner like you and me?'

'We are cleansed by blood, sir,' an older man responded with a loud voice.

'You are correct, my friend. In the Old Testament, a man was cleansed of sin by the blood of a lamb, which was killed as a sacrifice of atonement. It was an exchange where the purity and innocence of the spotless lamb would be transferred to you and your sin would be transferred to the lamb.'

John jumped down off the rock and began walking through the midst of the crowd.

'But these constant sacrifices,' John continued, 'were mere foreshadows of THE Lamb of God— Jesus Christ, the Righteous. You are I are cleansed of sin by faith alone in the finished work of Christ. He is your rock. He is your merit. He is your Lord. This morning, believe on the Lord Jesus Christ and you will be saved!'

Some of the men and women began crying and others began praying out loud. A breeze swept down the wooded slope and brought with it an array of fallen leaves swirling across the grass. It was as if the Holy Spirit himself was sweeping through the assembled crowd convicting them of sin and applying the work of Christ to their hearts.

Even though spies didn't find Bunyan preaching, that didn't mean the coast was clear. A national drama was unfolding and two political parties had emerged— each with very different views on how the country should be governed.

The Whigs wanted a combined monarch-parliament government, each with a certain amount of balanced power. They were open to Nonconformists and Puritans—like Bunyan—worshipping freely in England, mainly because they were extremely anti-

Catholic. To them Catholicism was idolatry and its head—the Pope—was the antichrist. In general, they wanted religious freedom (except for Catholics), a stronger Parliament and a decided Protestant church in England.

The Tories, on the other hand, favoured the absolute rule of the monarch. They wanted to keep the Episcopal-style church government and were generally more open to Catholics.

During the autumn of 1681, King Charles dissolved Parliament and proceeded to rule alone. Unchecked, the king could do as he wished whenever he wished. This move sent fear into the hearts of the Whigs, who watched their dreams of a balanced government crumble.

Bunyan, who had the backing of the Whigs, soon found himself once more at risk of imprisonment, or worse. But there was another issue that was on everybody's mind: who would replace King Charles when he died? The answer wasn't so simple.

The person who would naturally succeed Charles was his brother, James. But James was openly Catholic and such a thought brought dread and panic across the nation. Many believed that if James became King, he would wipe out all forms of Protestantism in the land and bring in Roman Catholicism as the only legal religion in England.

Thus, the Whigs wanted to exclude James from the throne and have James' Protestant daughter, Mary, to succeed Charles. The nation split; the Whigs on one side and the Tories on the other. Who would win?

'Run! Run! Run!' yelled a dirty young boy as he watched his older brother run around the bases. The whole team cheered and seemed to be jumping up and down in unison.

'Tagged! No points!' an older dark-haired boy said who had retrieved the cat and tagged the runner. Groans quickly blanketed the dusty Bedford field.

Despite the many variations of the game, tip-cat was still a beloved Sunday afternoon sport. The players were children of parents who usually did not go to church—they were 'sick' every Sunday morning.

As John concluded preaching for an assembly near Elstow, he set out on horse toward his own church in Bedford to follow up with some who were really sick in his congregation.

It was the same road which he had walked as a boy—pushing that wooden cart with dangling pots, pans and other metal wares. The thoughts of his childhood flooded his mind as he watched the summer sun peak above.

It wasn't long before John rounded a group of trees and saw the rowdy crowd. Even from a ways off, he knew what the boys were doing; he had been there before. But instead of quickly approaching them, he pulled on the reigns of his horse and just stopped on the road.

The road itself was quiet—Sundays usually were. 'Heavenly Father,' John said closing his eyes. 'How can

I possibly persuade these boys that they need Jesus Christ as their Lord and Saviour? That is probably the last thing on their minds right now. But I am reminded of how You convicted my own heart in the middle of a game of tip-cat and of the sin of breaking Your commandment to keep the Sabbath day holy. Would you strengthen me even now? Would you bring the lost children of this world to yourself? Amen.'

John looked back up at the sweaty boys and took a deep breath. Kicking the sides of his horse, he trotted for the dusty field off to the side of the road. As he approached, some of the boys noticed the rider coming toward them and the game came to a stop.

'Is that Mr Bunyan?' one of the boys asked out loud. Everyone knew who John was—he had become quite famous as a preacher and writer.

When he reached the side of the field, he jumped to the ground. 'Boys,' he called with a loud voice.

They all knew they were in trouble. It was one thing for one of their parents or even a layman from the church to say something to them, but it was quite another for John Bunyan himself—the renowned preacher—to specifically call them out.

John walked up to them and stopped. He glanced around and noticed a large oak tree a few hundred feet away. 'I want all of you to go over to that tree and sit down,' he said, pointing with his finger. The boys made haste toward the tree and sat in the green grass under its large branches. The shade was welcomed.

'Now you are probably thinking that you are in trouble,' he began with a smile. 'But do not worry. I want to tell you a story.'

The boys all looked at each other in confusion.

'You've seen the squirrels running around here gathering nuts for the winter. Well one squirrel was given the charge of collecting acorns while they were plenty, but instead of gathering acorns he decided to spend his time playing in the trees and splashing about in the cool pond.' Some of the boys grinned. 'Day after day, instead of collecting acorns, this little squirrel and some of his friends played and played.'

'Like us!' one of the younger boys said followed by hushed giggles.

'That is right, young lad,' John said, looking down at the boy. 'But while the squirrels were out playing, other animals came and took the acorns. Some of the acorns simply crumbled and withered away in the hot sun. As winter approached, our little squirrel got hungry and began searching for acorns. But he couldn't find any. They had all been taken.'

'What did he do?' one of the boys asked with a troubled voice.

'Well he looked under every tree and under every pile of leaves but none could be found.'

John knelt down so that he was eye level with the assembled boys. 'My friends, that little squirrel would not live to see another summer.'

The wide-eyed boys sat motionless in the grass and a gentle breeze rustled the leaves above.

'You see, lads, time ran out. Collecting acorns was not just what that squirrel was meant to do, but it was also the best thing for him. You and I have limited time on this earth and we have been given a charge—to love the Lord with all our heart, mind, soul and strength. But this task, this duty, is also best for us. For in pursuing Jesus Christ as the greatest Treasure in the universe, we are satisfied and fulfilled—beyond what any game, play or nut can provide.'

John continued. 'It is true that you are breaking the commandment to keep the Sabbath day holy. But more than that, pursuing the Lord on his day is the best thing for you. The Christian Sabbath has been given to you as a wonderful gift. Play is good, believe me. I love to play tip-cat. But time is running out and Jesus will come to judge the living and the dead. The commandments are there to strengthen our love for Jesus. Don't be like that squirrel and waste your life.'

At this, the boys all looked down and some began to cry. God had used John to share the good news of Jesus and, in doing so, had shared some heavenly acorns with some dying squirrels.

Pages went flying all over the ground. 'Pardon me,' the man said, speeding along toward St Paul's square.

John squatted down and began picking up the loose-leaf pages from the dirt. 'People are too rushed these days,' he thought to himself.

He piled them up again and held the stack of papers tightly against his chest as if he were now expecting somebody to bump into him. He was on his way to the print shop with his new book, which he titled *A Book for Boys and Girls*. After teaching the boys that summer under the tree, he decided to put together a book for children full of rhymes and meditations on the Christian life.

Finally, John made it into the print shop and handed the pages to a tall, thin man with a dark apron wrapped across his front. 'Here it is. I'm sorry that I am late. A man bumped into— '

'Let's see what we have here,' the man interrupted looking down at the first page.

> *When other children prayed*
> *That work I then delayed*
> *Ran up and down and played*
> *And thus from God have strayed.*

The man looked up at John. ''Tis very good, John.'
He kept reading.

> *Lord, Thou was crucified*
> *For sinners, bled and died*
> *I have, for Mercy, cried*
> *Let me not be denied.*

The man was pleased. 'I shall have it ready in no time.'

John walked out of the shop and took in a deep cool breath. It seemed like he was writing more and more these days. *A Book for Boys and Girls*, which he published in 1686, was his seventh book in five years. Between preaching each Sunday, ministering to the needs of his ever-growing church, working on metal projects in his shop and taking care of his family, Bunyan put out page after page of his studies, thoughts and sermons for the press.

His books were meeting a growing demand from people across England. A year earlier, in 1685, King Charles died leaving his Catholic brother, James, the King of England, Scotland and Ireland. Although James was more tolerant of Nonconformists and Puritans—like Bunyan—he was also more tolerant of Catholics. Before long, people everywhere feared that Protestantism would become illegal and that all who opposed Roman Catholicism would be persecuted.

Bunyan's books only strengthened public opposition against James. Like his brother, James was seen as an immoral ruler who loved women, sport and ale too much. For the upright Puritan, this fun-loving Catholic was not the most desirable monarch. Something had to happen. But what?

On the brink of inner turmoil and chaos, England braced itself for a shocking reality: King James would have to go.

Off to the Celestial City

John sat back and let the smell of the coffee house fill his nostrils. His friend William was in the middle of quizzing him...

'So do you know much about this covenant of redemption, John?' William asked resting his elbows on the thick wood table.

'I've read about it. It is the relationship between the Father and the Son before the world was created— that the Son would obey the law perfectly and redeem a people for the Father.'

The man's eyebrows raised up and down as John spoke and then rested in a confused state. 'But it is a relationship, right?'

'That is right, my friend,' John replied. 'The Trinity—Father, Son and Holy Ghost—is a mysterious relationship of three persons, yet one God. And we are called to be stewards of the mysteries of God, as St Paul tells us in First Corinthians.'

'How are we stewards of God's mysteries,' William enquired.

John smiled, sipped his coffee and leaned back in his chair. 'My William, you ask good questions. God has revealed himself through his holy Word, the Bible. But that is not the full revelation of himself or his will. We cannot understand God completely. We know in part, but one day, my friend, we will know in full. But for now, we have been given a precious gift to maintain, to uphold and to manage with humility. That is what I mean by being a steward.'

John spent many nights in the local coffee house, talking about theology and the Bible with people in his congregation, like William. You didn't have to be in a pulpit to preach - a coffee house did just as well.

This night was no different other than the fact that John felt unusually relaxed and at peace. The hanging lanterns throughout the coffee house gave a calming glow to the crowded room—broken only by the annoying outbursts of the smelly old man in the corner.

William, too, sat back in his chair and looked up at John. 'What do you think will happen to the king? I heard there is talk of invasion by William of Orange. Is that possible?'

William of Orange was married to the daughter of King James, Mary, and lived in the Netherlands. William and Mary were Protestant and were the celebrated hopefuls to 'rescue' England from the tyrannical and Catholic James.

'Yes, I heard that as well,' John said looking at some knife marks in the table. 'Whatever happens, God is sovereign and we must trust in his divine care.'

'John, may I ask a favour of you?'

'Yes, of course. What is it?' John replied leaning forward.

'It is my father. He lives in Reading and we have had a poor relationship for some time and I fear that he desires to disinherit me altogether. I have tried to write, but he does not write back. I have visited, but he is angry.'

'What do you want me to do?'

William hesitated. 'I want to talk with him again, but I would like you to talk with him first—to calm his anger and melt his heart.'

'Only the Spirit of God can do that,' John said with a small chuckle.

'Would you talk with him, John?'

'Of course, my friend. I shall leave in the morning.'

William's face brightened and he sat up as if a burden had just been lifted from his back. 'Thank you.'

The next morning, John woke up early and packed some cheese and bread in a small piece of cloth. The roosters began crowing and he looked to the eastern sky, which was painted red from the approaching sun.

Reading was around seventy miles southwest of Bedford and directly west of London. It would take John a good part of the day of riding, but John knew this was important for his neighbour and his life was a calling to service—of God and others.

John put the food and a light jacket in a leather satchel and started for the front door.

'Don't forget your Bible,' came a whispered voice from behind him.

John turned around. 'Thank you, dear,' John said taking it from Elizabeth's hand.

'When will you return?'

'Several days, Lord willing. I have been asked to preach at Mr Gamman's meeting-house near Whitechapel in London the day after next. So I will ride to London after meeting with Mr Hamilton.'

Elizabeth grabbed his hand and kissed it. 'Be safe.'

The ride to Reading was uneventful, but his mind raced as to how he would approach William's father and what he would say. It was not the kind of talk you want to have with someone—pointing out a particular sin like anger or pride. But somebody had to do it and John was committed.

When he arrived, he was surprised to see that the house was rather large. The front was brick and had painted columns supporting an awning.

John hopped off his horse and walked up to the front door and knocked.

'Mr Hamilton,' he called.

The door opened and a short, older man looked up at John.

'Mr Hamilton?'

'Yes, that is me. Who are you?'

'I am a neighbour of your son, William. My name is John Bunyan. May I come in?'

The man looked puzzled as if he should know the name. 'Do you write books?'

'Yes, I do.' Both of them paused for a few seconds. 'May I come in?' John asked again.

'Oh, yes. Please, come in.'

The two walked into what looked like a family room and sat down. 'May I get you something to drink?' the man asked, still with a puzzled look on his face.

'No, I am fine. Thank you.'

John cleared his throat and sat forward in his chair. 'I am here to talk about your relationship with your son.' He expected a quick response, but the man just kept staring back at him. 'He wants to talk with you, but fears that you would have nothing to do with him.'

'It has been a long time since we last spoke,' the man finally said, looking down. 'I have gotten old and it seems as though William does not want to care for me.'

The two talked well into the summer night about his relationship with his son until they both retired to bed. The conversation ended with joyful resolve and a hope-filled father longing to see his son.

The man showed John to a guest room on the second floor. As he lay in bed, he couldn't help but thank God for granting a soft heart to Mr Hamilton. 'Thank you, Lord. You have worked in this man's life tonight and I praise you and thank you for it!'

* * *

The next morning, John got up before the sunrise, ate some cheese and bread and started out the door before Mr Hamilton awoke. He left a letter expressing his gratitude and hopes for the reconciliation with his son.

When he walked out the front door, a heavy mist greeted him and John knew that this might be a long ride to London. With his leather satchel lashed to his saddle and a determined spirit, he began the forty-mile journey to London.

It was Saturday, 18 August 1688—a Saturday that had more in store for John than he would ever want. As soon as he began riding, the thick clouds suddenly burst open into heavy rain and John found himself completely exposed to the elements. For nearly five hours, John rode—drenched to the skin and cold. He remembered what his mother told him when he was young; how being out in the rain—even in the summer—could be very dangerous.

He finally reached the home of John Strudwick, a grocer and a fellow Nonconformist who lived on Snow Hill in London. The warm dry house was a welcomed treat.

'How is your church in Bedford, John?' Mr Strudwick asked. He himself was a deacon at a local Nonconformist congregation and wanted to know the state of the 'unofficial' church across England.

John moved a little closer to the fire and stretched out his hands. 'Difficult, my friend. You never know what service opportunities the Lord brings each day and Satan is quick to assault the faithful.'

'Very true.' Mr Strudwick sipped on some hot tea and propped one foot on a short stool in front of him. 'And your family, are they well?'

'Elizabeth and the children are well. My eldest daughter, Mary, died a few years ago. I loved her dearly.' John tucked his hands back under his armpits. 'She was blind, but had the sweetest frame and countenance. I miss her.'

'And you shall see her again. She is in a better place—a place where the blind will see.'

John smiled and looked over at Mr Strudwick. 'Thank you, my friend.' Standing up, John pulled a small wool blanket around his shoulders and turned his back to the fire. He felt a chill run down his spine and knew he needed to go to bed.

'I may sleep early, if that is fine with you. I am to preach tomorrow morning and need to be well-rested.'

Mr Strudwick stood up too. 'Yes, of course, John. Your room is down the hallway on the left. Let me know if you need anything else.'

Although he slept well through the night, he awoke with the same deep chill that reached to the very marrow of his bones. As he had promised, he rode to Mr Gamman's meeting-house and preached with an unusual earnestness and sense of conviction from

God's Word. He preached as though nothing at all troubled him. He preached as a dying man to dying men.

That evening, back at Mr Strudwick's house, John came down with a high fever. Sweat and tears seemed to be never-ceasing and the next day, Mr Strudwick sent a dispatch to Bedford, to Elizabeth.

Dear Mrs Bunyan,
Your husband is very sick and I believe it is best if you came to London soon. He is being taken care of, but I do not see any sign of improvement. Despite his illness, his heart and mind continue to soar with the Lord Jesus in almost unbroken communion. I know he would appreciate your tender affection.
Your servant in the Lord,
John Strudwick

Several days later, Elizabeth arrived. She left the children in the care of a few good families from the Bedford church. Hour after hour passed and John's fever only worsened.

Elizabeth sat on the edge of his bed with a cloth and small basin of water. 'John, can I get you anything— anything at all?' Elizabeth asked taking the cloth and wiping the sweat from his brow.

John didn't respond, but he opened his eyes and looked at her.

'I could open a window or bring some—'

'I am alright, Elizabeth. You have been faithful and constant in your gentle care and I love you.' John closed his eyes and coughed. 'I feel that the Lord is calling me home, calling me to cross the great River and to enter the eternal rest.'

As tears began to well up in Elizabeth's eyes, she wiped his brow once more. 'Then go, John. Enter your reward and I shall greet you again.'

And with that, John breathed his last and entered the Celestial City. It was 31 August 1688. He was buried three days later in Bunhill Fields, Finsbury, in a newly purchased vault owned by Mr Strudwick.

Four years later, Elizabeth did greet him again in glory. Their faith fastened them to the eternal Rock, Jesus Christ, who said, 'Come unto me, all ye who are weary and heavy laden and I will give thee rest.'

One month after John died, William and Mary landed at Torbey and James fled to France. Within a year, King William announced religious freedom to the whole of England. Nonconformists and Puritans alike would never feel the strain of persecution—as they did under Charles and James—again.

For a full list of Trailblazers, please see our website: www.christianfocus.com
All Trailblazers are available as e-books

John Bunyan:
Life Summary

John Bunyan lived from 1628 to 1688—a period of some of the most turbulent and momentous events in English history. At age fourteen, tensions erupted between Charles I and Parliament into a bloody civil war, which ended in the defeat and execution of the king. Under Oliver Cromwell, the whole structure of the Church of England was dismantled, leaving the Puritans in control of Parliament. But by 1660, the pendulum of national favour swung toward a monarchy and Charles II was crowned king—bringing with him the Restoration of the Church of England and persecution of the Puritans, like Bunyan. Bunyan endured the hardship of persecution, being confined in prison for over twelve years of his life, preaching in secret and often barely avoiding further imprisonment or execution.

Bunyan began his life as a tinker—working in his father's shop making and mending all sorts of metal wares. This was his primary trade until he was first imprisoned in 1660. But the tinker turned preacher and before he was released, he was known throughout England not only for his preaching, but also for his writing.

He preached, pastored a church in Bedford and wrote nearly sixty books and treatises. His most famous book was *The Pilgrim's Progress*. No other work in English, except the Bible, has been so widely read over such a long period. First published in 1678, the book has never been out of print and has been translated into over 200 languages. If ever a book deserved to be described as one of the 'world's classics,' it is *The Pilgrim's Progress*.

A humble man and a determined spirit, Bunyan laboured with his congregation in Bedford for over thirty-five years, even while he was imprisoned. His faithfulness to God's Word and influence across England earned him the nickname—ironically—'Bishop Bunyan.' When a fellow Nonconformist faced being fined, imprisonment or execution, it was John who stepped in to write letters and plead their case. He was a pastor to pastors and a friend of sinners.

The Pilgrim who found himself in the City of Destruction and losing his burden at the wicket gate, found himself struggling against both the power of the English crown and the power of Satan. But God was pleased to usher him into glory, into the Celestial City. To this day, we can find hope in the Lord's promise, even as we—one day—shall cross that great River:

Fear not, for I have redeemed you. I have summoned you by name; you are mine. As you pass through the waters, I will be with you; and when you pass through the rivers, they will not sweep over you. When you walk through the fire, you will not be burned; the flames will not set you ablaze. For I am the Lord, your God, the Holy One of Israel, your Saviour.

Isaiah 43:1-3

John Bunyan
Time Line

1628   John Bunyan born in Elstow, England

1633   William Laud appointed Archbishop of
        Canterbury.

1642   English Civil War begins at Battle of Edgehill.

1643   Westminster Assembly opens meetings.

1644   John's mother and sister die; father remarries
        within two months; John mustered in the
        parliamentary forces stationed in Newport
        Pagnell.

1645   Use of Prayer Book prohibited by Parliament.

1647   John returns to Elstow; *Westminster Confession of
        Faith* issued.

1648   John marries first wife, Mary, and sets up house
        in Elstow.

1649   Trial and execution of Charles I; England
        proclaimed a free commonwealth.

1650   John undergoes spiritual crisis lasting for nearly
        three years; first child, Mary, is born blind;
        receives counsel from John Gifford, pastor of an
        Independent church in Bedford.

1653   John becomes a member of Gifford's congregation
        in Bedford; Oliver Cromwell becomes 'Lord
        Protector' of England.

1655   John moves to Bedford and begins to preach.

1658	First wife dies; publishes first of his sermons.
1659	John marries second wife, Elizabeth.
1660	John is arrested for preaching illegally; Charles II becomes king.
1662	Act of Uniformity, requiring conformity to the newly published *Book of Common Prayer*.
1665	The Great Plague.
1666	The Great Fire of London.
1672	John is released from prison and becomes the pastor of the Bedford church.
1677	Imprisoned again for six months, writes *The Pilgrim's Progress*.
1678	Publishes *The Pilgrim's Progress*.
1685	Charles II dies and James II becomes king.
1688	John dies from a fever contracted from riding from Reading to London in heavy rain.
1689	William and Mary are proclaimed king and queen; Toleration Act grants freedom of worship to Protestant Nonconformists.

Thinking Further Topics

1. Raining Hard, Too Hard

Do you know someone who has died? It might have been a friend or family member. In this chapter, John's mother and sister died within two months of each other. John felt alone and angry, initially turning his anger and frustration toward God. He felt that God, if he was there at all, was simply causing pain and suffering in his life.

But death is a result of sin and sin entered the world through Adam and Eve's rebellion against God (Genesis 1–3). The Bible tells us in Romans 6:23 that 'the wages of sin is death,' which means that the natural result and punishment for our rebellion against God is death. That is why Adam and Eve were barred from the Tree of Life in Genesis 3.

But there is hope. Romans 6:23 goes on to say, 'but the gift of God is eternal life in Christ Jesus our Lord.' So wherever you are reading this, put your faith and hope in this 'gift.' God offers eternal life through his Son Jesus Christ if we but believe and trust in him.

2. Guns, Smoke and God

This chapter describes John's experience in the English Civil War (1642-48). He was called to arms, fighting with the Parliamentary army against King Charles I. But there was a deeper war going on in his own heart and mind – a spiritual war.

Do you ever feel that there is a 'war' going on inside you as well? Perhaps you find yourself battling against a certain sin in your life over and over again? Maybe you struggle with the temptation to doubt God's goodness or even his existence. You are not alone.

The Apostle Paul tells us in Ephesians 6:12 that our real battle 'is not against flesh and blood, but against the rulers, against the authorities, against the powers of this dark world and against the spiritual forces of evil in the heavenly realms.' You see, Satan and his host of demons are set on trying to destroy you and that is why Paul goes on to exhort us to 'put on the full armour of God.'

Ultimately, we are to put on Jesus Christ. That means that we trust in Jesus' life, death and resurrection on our behalf! Only when we are clothed in Jesus' righteousness are we found faultless and protected from Satan and his evil snares.

So, today, put on the full armour of God and stand firm trusting not in your own abilities or righteousness, but only in the worth and merit of Jesus Christ, the Saviour of sinners.

3. Chief of Sinners!

John always seemed to get into trouble as a teenager. Although he did quite well at dodging blame and punishment, people knew him as a trouble-maker and rebel. But as time went on, God began to show him his sin and John started desiring God and desiring knowledge of his Word, the Bible.

Even though John knew what was right and good, he felt like the temptation to sin was greater and found himself in trouble again and again. It was almost as if his heart desired the things of God, but his weak flesh pulled him back into sin every time.

Do you ever feel like, deep down, you want to do what's right, but your sinful nature and weakness pulls you back into succumbing to temptation? The Apostle Paul did. In Romans 7:18-19, Paul explains his desperate situation: 'I have the desire to do what is good, but I cannot carry it out. For what I do is not the good I want to do; no, the evil I do not want to do—this I keep on doing.'

If you find yourself in this situation, where you don't feel like you can do the good that you want to do, there is hope and forgiveness at the cross of Christ. For Paul concludes this desperate situation by giving us one of the greatest promises in the Bible. Romans 8:1 says, 'Therefore, there is now no condemnation for those who are in Christ Jesus.' Meditate on this verse and let its truth sink into your heart and soul. If you are in Christ (believing in his death for your sins), you are declared 'not guilty' by God. Despite your weakness, despite your sin, you can stand freed by Jesus' payment on your behalf. Go forth, then, with confidence that your sins have been covered by the blood of the eternal Saviour.

4. Family Names and Sunday Games

In this chapter, John struggled with keeping the fourth commandment in the Bible: 'Remember the Sabbath day by keeping it holy' (Exodus 20:8). Like most people, John worked six days of the week. He was a tinker, making pots and pans and fixing other metal objects for people. When Sunday came around, John felt like that was his day, not the Lord's. He wanted to play and have fun—not pray, worship or learn his catechism.

Christians today usually worship on Sunday because that is the day when Christ rose from the dead and when his first followers met to worship and take communion together. The word 'sabbath' means rest. So the Christian Sabbath—Sunday—is a day of rest where we are to cease from normal day-to-day activities and rest in our Lord Jesus and his work on our behalf.

What do your Sundays look like? Do they look different from any other day of the week? The reason we are to set Sunday apart from the others is so that we can take a day to focus on God. God knows our sinful hearts and busy lives enough to know that if he didn't set apart a day for us to enjoy him, it wouldn't happen at all.

The Sabbath was given as a gift for us to enjoy the goodness of God, to worship him and to meditate on the gift of his Son, Jesus. Take advantage of this gift. Jesus says in Matthew 11:28, 'Come to me, all you who are weary and burdened, and I will give you rest.' Jesus offers you rest. Come and find rest in him today and taste and see that the Lord is good.

5. Thank You, John Gifford!

Have you ever had a friend or family member who has been a great influence on you - spending quality time with you? In this chapter, a pastor named John Gifford took young Bunyan under his wing. He mentored him, spent time with him and pointed Bunyan to the gospel of Jesus Christ.

In the Bible, the Apostle Paul had this kind of relationship with a young Christian named Timothy. He viewed Timothy as a son addressing him as 'Timothy, my true son in the faith.' Paul taught Timothy about the gospel and the Christian life and how to be a leader and mentor to others.

Another thing that Paul told Timothy was not to let anyone look down on him because he was young (1 Timothy 4:12). Though Timothy was young, he was to step up and lead. You might be thinking that you are too young to be a Christian leader in your church or community. But God tells us to set an example in speech, life, faith, love and purity (1 Timothy 4:12)—no matter what your age.

Think of somebody that you might be able to mentor or disciple. God may be asking you to step up and be a leader for him and for his church. Now think again about somebody who has taken you under their wing, take a few minutes and write him or her a thank-you note. They deserve it!

6. Preach the Word!

In this chapter, John decided to move from Elstow to Bedford with his family. It was a hard decision and one that took great courage and faith. John didn't know exactly what would be in store for him and his family, but he felt that that was where God was leading them to live and to work.

Have you ever had to move from one place to another? Or have you ever had to make a decision that would put you into an uncomfortable or unfamiliar place where you don't know anybody?

In the book of Genesis, Abraham was asked to leave his home land of Haran and travel to the unknown land of Canaan. By faith, he followed the Lord and he and his family packed up and moved. God eventually gave Canaan to Abraham's offspring, the Israelites, which is where they are today.

The next time you find yourself having to make a difficult transition or you are afraid, trust that God is watching over you. In fact, his love for you is so great that if you think on his love, it dissolves your fear like sugar in hot tea. First John says that 'perfect love drives out fear.' Remember God's love for you for you are his adopted son or daughter. It is true that 'nothing will separate you from his love' (Romans 8:39)!

7. Ink, Paper and the Quakers

Some people were taking part of the gospel and knitting it together with their own ideas and, in turn, had created a new religion called Quakerism. Quakerism believed that all people had an 'inner light' to guide them. They are to follow this inner light, even if it was contrary to what the Bible said. Bunyan was forced to step up and defend the truths of Scripture against heresy.

Have you ever heard a sermon on television or the radio or even in a church where the preacher said something that just didn't sound like it was coming from the Bible? Or maybe the preacher did the opposite—he didn't preach what the Bible plainly stated. This often happens today where many preachers do not talk about sin or the suffering of Jesus because it is too offensive and it might hurt peoples' feelings.

The Galatian church in the Bible was beginning to believe in a 'gospel' that was really not the gospel at all. Paul writes in Galatians 1:9, 'If anyone is preaching to you a gospel other than what you accepted [from us], let him be eternally condemned!' You might be thinking that these words are a bit harsh. But what is worse? To believe a false, inoffensive gospel and go to eternal hell or to believe an offensive, but true gospel and enjoy eternal life with the Saviour?

Increasingly, the church is coming under attack and there may be a time in your life when you will need to defend the Word of God and the gospel of Jesus Christ. And when you do, remember to do so in humility and compassion for you were saved by God's grace alone so you have no room to boast.

8. Arrested!

This chapter shows the events surrounding John's imprisonment. He spent twelve years in gaol, suffering cold winters, awful smells, lack of food and the loneliness of not living with his family.

You probably haven't had suffering like this before, but if you have you are not alone. There are people dying everyday because they believe in Jesus Christ as their Lord. They are tortured, beaten and killed for simply identifying themselves with the Saviour. How did John find hope in such horrible circumstances? How do people endure the pain of suffering for Christ's sake?

Paul tells us in chapter 3 of Philippians that everything in this world is worthless compared to the surpassing greatness of knowing Jesus Christ. He goes on in verse 10, 'I want to know Christ and the power of his resurrection and the fellowship of sharing in his sufferings, becoming like him in his death.' Did you see that? He wants to know the fellowship of sharing in Christ's sufferings! Paul wanted to be identified with Christ so much that he could say, as he did earlier in Philippians 1:21, 'For to me, to live is Christ and to die is gain.'

Whatever trials you have gone through, are going through or may go through in the future, be assured that Christ has endured and suffered more. In our sufferings, we can identify with the Suffering Servant, who, for the joy that was set before him, endured the cross (Hebrews 12:2). Look to him as your Saviour and rejoice in the salvation he has prepared for you!

9. Shivering with Shoelaces

Have you ever been on the losing team in a sport? Have there been times when your grades at school weren't as good as some of your friends' grades? You probably were hurt or maybe embarrassed. But whatever your feelings were, you gained a sense that—at least to some extent— you were weak. You weren't as strong as you wanted to be or as smart as you hoped. But did it ever occur to you that such a sense of weakness might actually be a good thing?

In his gaol cell, John felt completely helpless and weak. He felt vulnerable and a little scared. He didn't know the future and didn't have a way to provide for his family other than making one shoelace at a time. But in the midst of his weakness, God reminded him of a passage from 2 Corinthians, chapter 12. Jesus spoke to the Apostle Paul and told him, 'My grace is sufficient for you, for my power is made perfect in weakness' (12:9). Paul concluded that he would boast all the more gladly in his weaknesses, so that the power of Christ might rest upon him.

The amazing thing about the gospel is that Christ looks more glorious and wonderful in your weakness because it shows that Jesus didn't save you for being the best-looking or the smartest or the fastest. He saves sinners who are desperate and weak. He saves sinners who need a Saviour.

Next time you fall upon a situation where your weakness is highlighted, rejoice and look to the all-satisfying Saviour who promises that his grace is sufficient for you.

10. The Preacher Released

As you are reading this, think about the gifts God has given you. You might be a good musician or perhaps a good football player. Did you know that God has given gifts to you so that you can serve others and honour him? As you catalogue your gifts, do you find yourself serving others with them and honouring God? This might be a good time of reflecting and evaluating your priorities.

John's gift was preaching. Not only did he feel the call of God to preach, others testified to his gift and encouraged him to keep it up. God tells us in 1 Peter 4:10, 'Each one should use whatever gift he has received to serve others, faithfully administering God's grace in its various forms.' John used his gift of preaching and God was glorified. Many came to believe in Christ as Lord and Saviour through his preaching.

Your gift might not be preaching, but it might be your mind if you are a good student at school. How can you use your mind to serve others and glorify God? How can you use your athletic abilities to serve others and glorify God? How can you use your musical talents to serve others and glorify God?

First Peter goes on to say, 'Whoever serves, serve by the strength that God supplies—in order that in everything God may be glorified through Jesus Christ. To him belong glory and dominion forever and ever. Amen.' May that be your chief end—to glorify God in your life and gifts!

11. The Perilous Progress of a Pilgrim

This chapter tells the story of John being arrested a second time and describes the events surrounding the writing of *The Pilgrim's Progress*. The work, which has never been out of print since 1678 and has sold more copies than any other book in the English language (with the exception of the Bible), became an instant success across England.

The book tells the story of a man named Christian who journeys through perilous situations but in the end, reaches the Celestial City, which symbolizes heaven. Among the many significant truths found in the book, one stands out—God preserves his people until the very end.

You might wonder whether or not you will go to heaven. It's a good question to think about. It's been asked before, 'On a scale of 1 to 10, ten being absolutely certain, how sure are you that you will go to heaven when you die?' Most people who go to church will usually say 6 or 7 because they think that they could always improve or do more or they think that they are not good enough.

But that's the point! You aren't good enough; Christ is...for you. Going to heaven doesn't depend on how 'good' you are. It depends on the work of Christ. All that is required of us is to believe in him. Jesus says in John 6:37: 'All that the Father gives me will come to me, and whoever comes to me I will never drive away.'

Take comfort in knowing that your weak faith doesn't make Christ any less your righteousness. If you trust in Jesus, you will go to heaven. Now that that is settled, we freely live in obedience to God and his Word out of love and joy.

12. The Tables Turn

John was released again from gaol and was allowed to travel all over to preach and teach God's Word. This chapter shows how God used John to build up and grow the church across England.

But although Bunyan was faithful to God in using his gifts to serve others and glorify God, it was God himself who converted sinners and gave them Jesus.

In a very important passage in Matthew 16:16 Peter confesses that Jesus is 'the Christ, the Son of the living God.' Immediately, Jesus tells him that 'on this rock, I will build my church, and the gates of hell shall not prevail against it.' This should give you joy and comfort. Despite the onslaught of attack upon the church, despite the plans of Satan to bring down God's people through temptation and suffering, Jesus Christ will build his church!

There may have been times in your life—maybe at school or with friends—that you have been ashamed of Jesus. It may be hard to admit, but it might be true that at one time or another, you didn't want to be associated with him for fear of rejection or fear that somehow your witness might actually damage the growth of Christ's church.

But take heart; Christ will build his church. That is his promise and he is King of kings and Lord of lords, the eternal Son, the Alpha and Omega. He will build his church and the very gates of hell cannot stand in its way. If you trust in him, you are considered his glorious bride whom he loves and for whom he has given his life. Keep your chin up; you have the Champion on your side!

13. Off to the Celestial City

Even at the very end of his life, John is still working for the cause of the gospel. In this chapter, he travels to Reading in order to reconcile a broken relationship between a father and son. After talking with the father, he heads back to Bedford, stopping in London on the way. But on his ride to London, he gets caught in heavy rain, which causes a high fever—a fever from which John never recovered.

In the United States, there is something called the 'American Dream.' It says that if you are making a lot of money, have an easy life and do whatever it is that makes you happy…then you are living the American Dream. Many even dream of retiring early just to spend the rest of life watching butterflies or sailing on a big yacht.

But this is such a sad life! On the other hand you have John Bunyan, the Apostle Paul or even Jesus himself— giving their lives for the sake of others and for the glory of God, even until the very end.

Don't waste your life! Make each moment count. The American Dream has left people empty and still dreaming. Make your life goal not to be happy, but to glorify and enjoy God. Then you can say with Paul, 'I have fought the good fight, I have finished the race, I have kept the faith' (2 Timothy 4:7). One day, you too will join Bunyan, Paul and Christ himself in your heavenly home—the Celestial City.

Christian Focus Publications publishes books for adults and children under its four main imprints: Christian Focus, CF4K, Mentor and Christian Heritage. Our books reflect our conviction that God's Word is reliable and Jesus is the way to know him, and live for ever with him.

Our children's publication list includes a Sunday School curriculum that covers pre-school to early teens, and puzzle and activity books. We also publish personal and family devotional titles, biographies and inspirational stories that children will love.

If you are looking for quality Bible teaching for children then we have an excellent range of Bible stories and age-specific theological books.

From pre-school board books to teenage apologetics, we have it covered!

Find us at our web page:
www.christianfocus.com